309.175        ASC 19300
DYE      Dyer, G.W.

~~Democracy in the south~~
~~before the Civil War.~~

~~Agnes Irwin School~~
~~Upper School Library~~

# The American South

# The American South

SEVEN BOOKS SUGGESTED
FOR REPRINTING BY
C. VANN WOODWARD

G. W. Dyer
*Democracy in the South Before the Civil War.* 1905

D. R. Hundley
*Social Relations in Our Southern States.* 1860

Charles H. Otken
*The Ills of the South, Or, Related Causes Hostile
to the General Prosperity of the Southern People.*
1894

Robert Royal Russel
*Economic Aspects of Southern Sectionalism, 1840–1861.*
1923

Robert Somers
*The Southern States Since the War, 1870–1.* 1871

D. Augustus Straker
*The New South Investigated.* 1888

Richard Taylor
*Destruction and Reconstruction: Personal Experiences
of the Late War.* 1879

# DEMOCRACY IN THE SOUTH
# BEFORE THE CIVIL WAR

BY G. W. DYER

## ARNO PRESS

A NEW YORK TIMES COMPANY

New York ☆ 1973

Reprint Edition 1973 by Arno Press Inc.

Reprinted from a copy in
  The State Historical Society of Wisconsin Library

The American South
ISBN for complete set: 0-405-05058-5

Manufactured in the United States of America

———◆———

Library of Congress Cataloging in Publication Data

Dyer, G    W
    Democracy in the South before the Civil War.

    (The American South)
    Reprint of the ed. published by Publishing House of
the Methodist Episcopal Church, South, Nashville.
    1. Southern States--Social conditions.  2.  Southern
States--Economic conditions.  3.  Education--Southern
States.  I.  Title.  II.  Series.
HN79.A13D94  1973        309.1'75'03        72-11343
ISBN 0-405-05059-3

# DEMOCRACY IN THE SOUTH BEFORE THE CIVIL WAR.

BY G. W. DYER, M.A.,

*Instructor in Economics and Sociology in Vanderbilt University, Nashville, Tenn.*

NASHVILLE, TENN., AND DALLAS, TEX.:
PUBLISHING HOUSE OF THE METHODIST EPISCOPAL CHURCH, SOUTH.
SMITH & LAMAR, AGENTS.

# PREFACE.

This study is a compendium of a more comprehensive work which will be published later. If some of the conclusions drawn are not supported by sufficient data, the reader is asked to withhold his verdict until the more intensive study is examined.

# TABLE OF CONTENTS.

# INTRODUCTORY.

1. Democracy in the South before the Civil War.

Democracy is here used in its broadest sense. It has reference not only to the political life of the South, but also to the industrial, the social, and the educational life as well.

"Democracy has been a movement toward the emancipation of the individual. Democratic evolution is essentially the evolution of the recognition of the individual on his merits as an individual." Society is democratic to the extent that the social organism, as far as possible, gives to each individual an opportunity to develop all the normal powers with which he has been endowed. The passion of Democracy is to give to each individual as good an opportunity as is possible, in an imperfect world, to do the best work of which he is capable, and also to give to each the full reward of his work.

Then to what extent was the individual freeman, as an individual, recognized in the South before the Civil War? What opportunities, if any, were given here to the poor man to rise on his merits? Was the Southern poor man kept down by hindrances which were not in existence to the same extent in other sections of this country? To what extent did poor men actually rise to places of honor and trust in the South? Were the great masses of the people under the domination of an aristocratic oligarchy, or did the people have a voice in the government under which they lived? If there was a proud aristocratic oligarchy in the South that ruled in every sphere of life, how did this oligarchy get control and keep control over the great masses of people? What was the general character of the white population? What was the general character of the social, political, industrial, and educational life of the South?

These are some of the questions which the writer has tried to answer in the pages that follow.

In this study the writer has had two objects in view. In the first place, he has tried to make a limited investigation of Democracy

in the South before emancipation.  In the second place, he has
attempted to show that the methods used by our leading historians
are most defective, and that these writers have grossly misrepre-
sented the life of the Southern people.

## 2. The Interpretation of Social Phenomena.

Is there any history to which we may turn and get a true picture
of life in the South before the Civil War?  Many give us glimpses
of the truth, but where can we get the political life, the social life,
the educational life, the industrial life, the religious life just as it
was?  This the writer does not believe has yet been written, either
in histories or elsewhere.  Certainly he has not found it.  He has
not examined all that has been written, however, and hence his
criticism must be limited to the field of his investigation.

The true work of the historian has been well stated by Mr. Her-
bert Spencer.  "That which constitutes history properly so called,"
says Mr. Spencer, "is in great part omitted from works on this
subject.  Only of late years have historians commenced giving us,
in any considerable quantity, the truly valuable information.  As
in past ages the king was everything and the people nothing, so in
past history the doings of the king filled the entire picture, to
which the national life forms but an obscure background; while
only now, when the welfare of nations rather than of rulers is be-
coming the dominant idea, are historians beginning to occupy themselves with the phenomena of social progress.  The thing it really
concerns us to know is the natural history of society.  We want all
facts which help us to understand how a nation has grown and
organized itself."

The leading American historians of recent years seem to have in
substance the conception of their mission as outlined by Mr. Spencer,
as far as the subject-matter of their work is concerned; and for
this they deserve our sincere congratulations.  This distinction did
not belong to their predecessors.  The earlier historians of the
United States seemed to have thought that their sole mission was
to tell of wars, detail battles, "and curse out England."  At any
rate this is about all they did.  While the historians of recent years
have justly won for themselves a commendable distinction in their
conception of the proper subject-matter of history, in the gathering
and in the arrangement of data in the relation of cause and effect,

which is also the function of the historian, they have fallen far short of the mark.

The writer does not take the extreme position that every single history of the United States misrepresents the facts of Southern life. As stated before, he has not read all the histories of the United States. There may be small histories and other similar productions that give the truth as far as they go, but in them he has good reasons to believe that only a very small part of the truth has been told. His criticisms, however, will be confined to the more prominent writers and historians; and these he does not claim have been altogether wrong in their interpretation of life in the South. Such a position would certainly be untenable. His position is, that the facts stated by them, and the inductions properly made, are only a part of what they have stated as facts and correct generalizations; and since they have failed to put in quotation marks, or otherwise brand the statements and positions not yet established, we are forced to be extremely skeptical with regard to any and everything they say.

To interpret correctly social phenomena is extremely difficult. Perhaps no science demands more in scientific training and in native capacity of those who write in any way authoritatively of its phenomena than is demanded of the man who presumes to interpret for us the life of the people in any locality. Yet, here and there all over the country, we find men and women, who have had little or no scientific training in any department of knowledge, and certainly none in the social and kindred sciences, writing and speaking dogmatically on the most intricate and complicated problems of societary life. These people have little or no data; they ignore data. The dogmatic assertions of these ignorant or disordered or prejudiced minds appear in our histories and other books and periodicals, sometimes under the sensational titles, "Mr. So-and-So on the South," or on "The Race Problem of the South," or on "The Poor Whites of the South," or on "The Negro in the South," etc.

No other evidence is needed to establish the fact that we are in a deplorably chaotic state with reference to the interpretation of social phenomena than the "stuff" that has been written and published and read and believed in our day on conditions in the South. The result is, the people of the North and of the rest of the world, and even the Southern people, have been confused, befuddled, and misled into all kinds of errors with reference to Southern conditions both in the past and at the present time.

Those who accept as true the account given in our leading histories of life in the South before the war know little more of the real conditions than the ancients knew of the science of astronomy, and not so much as the higher critics claim to know about the life of the Jews three thousand years ago. The census reports of the United States and some other documents of a similar nature, which, it would seem, almost no one has examined critically, are about the only records known to the writer than can be relied on at all to give the true conditions in the South either before or since the war.

To-day everybody may write, and anybody may be taken as authority. Such a state of things is always found in any sphere where quackery rules supreme. Since very little has been scientifically and positively established, any man or woman, regardless of race, color, or previous conditions of servitude, regardless of education, opportunities for observations, or scientific training, may interpret for us the most complicated social conditions, and may have their interpretations accepted as true by a large number of intelligent people. Whether that which is written is accepted as the correct interpretation, in many cases, is not determined by the truth or reasonableness of the statements, neither by the sanity of the writer, but by the writer's hypnotic power in psychic manipulation. In such a state the man who writes intelligently often fails to get a hearing, while the fanatic, the juggler, the impostor is made a hero. The quack doctor, who is generally a practical psychologist, understands very thoroughly this trait in human nature, and hence allows his hair to grow long, and paints his face, and in other ways looks as eccentric as possible in order that he may get a hearing and sell his "conjurations," and he succeeds; so do others succeed.

If a man in this day writes a treatise on toad frogs or June bugs or grasshoppers, or earthworms (and most of us are very familiar with these animals) without giving evidence of a thoroughly scientific knowledge of the subject discussed, no reputable periodical would publish it unless the editor desire to give an object lesson of the intense ignorance of the present day. We have a very strict censorship on what goes out to the world through the press on "toad frogs" and "earthworms," but anything may be published from anybody on the most difficult and the most important of all the problems of this world, the problem of human society.

A man jumps on a train somewhere in the North, in some cases, perhaps, with his conclusions carefully written out, and properly signed before he leaves home, and dashes through some section of the South, stopping a day here and possibly two days there, talking with hotel clerks and a few others equally as wise, who may be as deeply prejudiced and almost as ignorant as our "lightning express historian," and then hurries back to write up the South. He tells us of the industrial problem of the South, the race problem, the social problem, and every other problem. It is not necessary to say that this man has had no scientific training in his subject: his productions are adequate proof of this. The fact that he writes at all knowingly, is sufficient proof that he is a quack. But in many cases he does not get on a train at all, although the trains are running every day and the fare is cheap; somebody else got on the train years ago and told a man who told him that these inductions were true. In some cases, it would seem that nobody got on the train, but that our writer formed his inductions out of the abundance of his own ignorance. It was said of a certain man in Congress some years ago that every time he spoke something was subtracted from the sum total of human knowledge. This has certainly taken place when some have spoken of conditions in the South. These "lightning express historians and sociologists" know about as much about the phenomena they presume to interpret as a man would know about general fish life in the Atlantic Ocean simply from having passed across in a fast steamer. If these writers would be content to give us simply the facts they have observed, perhaps they would do no great harm. But the serious charge we bring against them is, they give us what they did not see and could not have seen.

But another writer, this time from the South, speaks dogmatically of the people with whom he is acquainted, and among whom he has lived all his life; in fact, he is one of them. Surely he may be trusted to give us the truth, especially when he shows his "cosmopolitanism" by taking a position antagonistic to the opinions and traditions of his own people, thus making a martyr of himself at home and a hero of himself abroad; surely such a one gives the true inductions, many seem to think. If such a writer would confine himself to his own little community in the South, and to his own little field of observation, his assertions, perhaps, would deserve some consideration. But this he rarely does; he talks about the "South!" The very strong probability is that he is utterly incapable of interpreting even the life of his own little community. In the first place the presumption is against the man rather than in his favor who takes a position antagonistic to the opinions and traditions of the best and most intelligent people of his community; and in the second place such a man is in greater danger of going to an extreme than a man from the outside world. The most extreme Democrat is often the man who was "brought up" a Republican, and vice versa. Colonel Ingersoll was the son of a good Presbyterian preacher. But the fact that a man lives in a community, whatever may be his feelings or opinions, is no proof whatever that he can interpret correctly the life of that community. One man thinks that he with a very few others, who agree with him in theology, are the only real Christians in his community. Many other Christians of the same community do not agree with him. One man thinks the mayor of his town is giving the people the best administration they have ever had, and another man thinks it is the worst. One man thinks that his neighbors are kind, generous, and brotherly; another thinks that the same neighbors are the opposite. One man thinks that education has been a blessing to the negroes around him, and another, in the same community, thinks that it has been a curse. Mr. Mitchell thinks that labor organization has proved a great blessing to the miners of the anthracite coal region, while Mr. Baer thinks it has been the worst kind of a curse. One man thinks that the great masses around him were never so well off as to-day, and hence should be happy and contented, while another man living in a stone's throw of the first, perhaps on the same street, thinks that these same people are in the worst kind of slavery, and he is almost ready to lead a revolution to emancipate them. The rule is, we accept those interpretations that please us, regardless of the interpreter, and those we do not like we reject. The result is, we have as many "histories" and "sociologies" as we have persons of different tastes. As a matter of fact, very, very few people are at all capable of interpreting the social conditions that immediately surround them; and much less are they capable of interpreting conditions in outside communities, and the conditions that surrounded past generations. Geological inductions, made by one not scientifically trained in geology, from phenomena which he has seen and felt and handled all his life, would not be accepted at all, even by a tenth-rate scientist of this department; and it is not nearly so difficult to make correct inductions in this field as it is in the sphere of social phenomena; yet here everybody is a trained expert who presumes to write.

Through such a state of quackery the science of medicine, as well as every other science, has had to pass. There was a time, and not so long ago, when the scientific physician was at a discount in many localities, and when almost every old woman in the community was a "doctor." These "skilled" physicians could make an absolutely perfect diagnosis of any case of sickness, however serious and complicated, at first sight; and could prescribe at once an equally perfect remedy which would surely restore, in a very short while, the unfortunate patient unless the "good Lord" had decided to call him home. In those days mourners and undertakers did a thriving business, for many were "called."

Then who may be heard in this field? What inductions from social phenomena may be accepted as established beyond a reasonable doubt? We certainly cannot accept as established what the great majority believe. The great majority once believed that the earth was the center of the universe. The great majority believe to-day that "Free Silver" is the best monetary policy, and to-morrow it is not. They believe to-day that the high protective tariff has been one of the strongest factors of our national progress, and a great blessing to the masses; and to-morrow that it has been a stubborn impediment to our progress, and a curse to the masses. The great majority believe to-day that the negro is the equal of the Anglo-Saxon, politically, socially, and every other way, and that he is eminently fitted not only to govern himself, but to govern the Anglo-Saxon also; but to-morrow they are not quite so sure. Neither can we accept as established what the "most intelligent" believe. The "most intelligent," like the "great majority," have defended all kinds of fallacies, and believed all kinds of foolish things. Neither can we accept the inductions of the "best people" of any community. The "best people" once burned witches at the stake, and are continually building fires around the innocent. "Surely we may accept as established what the 'well-informed' tell us," some one may say. No, the "well-informed" cannot be trusted to give us the truth. Men may study social phenomena all their lives, and at last be farther from the truth than the man who has studied but little. Karl Marx was well-informed; so is Herr Most. All depends on the methods used by the "well-informed" in reaching his conclusions, and on his opportunity and capacity for seeing all the facts germane to his subject. Can the novelist be trusted to give us history? The novelist is primarily an artist, and not a scientific student of society. He may tell us what really did exist, or he may tell us simply what he thinks may or might have existed. Grant that he is true to nature. This simply means that there lived in the community, where the plot is laid, men and women like the characters he represents, and that the phases of life he gives us were also found there. But since we can find almost any kind of characters, and any kind of life, anywhere, the novelist is worth but little to us in giving us the true life of the whole people. How far his characters are representative of the people in general of the community, and how far the phases of life given are representative of the whole life of the people, and how far this community is representative of adjacent communities, we cannot tell until we learn more about the conditions than the novelist knows, and then we do not need his interpretation. But it is conceding too much to grant that the novelist is always true to nature. He often has a purpose in view which may, and as a rule does, lead him to greatly exaggerate his characters and scenes for artistic and other effects. Novels and other writings of fiction are to be taken only as suggestive of what may have been or may be by him who would know the real social conditions. They have no place in historical or sociological libraries.

The reader will observe the difference between "induction" and the "simple statement of fact." There is a wide difference between the two, and one not always observed. Any man of ordinary common sense, who has a good reputation in his community for truth and veracity, must be accepted as a competent witness in his simple statement of facts of his own knowledge. However, it is not at all uncommon that such a man is flatly contradicted by another witness equally as competent. Then, even in the mere statement of facts, good men are often very far from the truth. But to refuse to give weight to the simple statement of fact by a competent witness is to discredit the witness unjustly, and bring a serious charge against his character. But to refuse to accept his inductions is no reflection on his character (as a matter of fact the courts will not allow the best and most intelligent man in the community, as a witness, to make inductions at all, except in rare cases), but is simply a reflection on him as a trained expert—a logician—a scientist in the particular specialty whose phenomena he presumes to interpret. He may be a recognized authority, or at least in good repute, in other departments of science and a quack in sociology; and such cases, we are sorry to say, are not uncommon in our day. Such men, we believe, are more in the way of the scientific study of society than almost any others, since their ability and prestige in their special departments give them a hearing, among the uninformed, which is out of all proportion to their real knowledge.

The difference between the man with the truly scientific spirit (and not all so-called scientists have the scientific spirit) and the quack, in any sphere of knowledge, is, the one makes his theory conform to every known fact, while the other makes every known fact conform to his theory; the one diligently searches for and takes cognizance of all attainable facts bearing on the subject, while the other searches for and takes cognizance of only those facts that will aid him in establishing his preconceived conclusions; the one states what he believes to be the truth, the whole truth, and nothing but the truth, while the other states that, and only that, which will make his theory seem plausible; the one states positively only that which is known to be true, while the other states positively that which might have been true, or that which he thinks ought to have been true, as though it were established; the one cannot consciously mislead the people, while the other thinks the end justifies the means, and hence can mislead the people with impunity; the one loves the truth better than he loves his theories, while the other loves his theories better than he loves the truth. Not all quacks can be characterized in the above way; many are honest and conscientious, but are simply ignorant, and don't know enough to know when a thing is established.

The really competent interpreter of social phenomena is he who has the desire to see, the capacity to see, the scientific training to see, the opportunity to see, and the energy to see all that can be seen that is relevant to the subject of his investigation. In addition to this he must have the willingness and the capacity to give every fact that is germane to his subject its proper place in his inductions, and the honesty and love of truth that will compel him to state all that truth demands, and nothing more.

The fact that one making an investigation has at the beginning of his work a strong desire which may be characterized as a prepossession or bias or prejudice, that the final conclusions reached should be favorable to some party concerned, does not necessarily unfit him for the best scientific work. Perhaps every one who begins the investigation of any important social question (as well as nearly every other question) has some such feeling, though he is not always conscious of it. All other things being equal, the man without bias is most competent for such investigations. But sometimes the fact that a man feels deeply, and is strongly desirous that the conclusions reached should establish certain facts, may be of real service to him in reaching the best scientific results. Such a feeling at the beginning of his work will tend to make him work the harder, and make his investigations the more thorough. If he be dishonest and love his bias better than the truth, of course he is incompetent; but if he be honest and really desire to know the truth and follow the truth, above everything else in this world, he is competent as far as this point is concerned. In properly criticising conclusions reached by the scientific method, in any department of knowledge, what the one who drew the conclusion believed or felt at any period of his life does not constitute an essential element of his data; for, apart from this, he is obligated to furnish us data, which may be known by all, sufficient to establish his conclusions. It is only in the fields of quackery that we are compelled to know the psychology of the writer before we know how to accept what he states.

The really essential qualifications of the competent interpreter of social phenomena are that he have the scientific spirit, which is the spirit of truth, and that he follow the scientific method, which is the method of reason. He who has these, whatever else he may have or may not have, deserves to be heard; he who is without them, whatever his other qualifications, is incompetent.

But it may be said that history is not a science, and hence the same rules cannot be applied in the interpretation of social phenomena that are applied in the interpretations of the phenomena of a recognized science, as chemistry or geology, or biology. Granting all this to be true, it does not follow at all that the scientific method cannot be applied in the interpretation of its phenomena. On the other hand, it is now conceded by scientists in general, I think, that the scientific method should be used in the investigation of all phenomena.

At the present time we are compelled to confess that we know but little accurately about social phenomena, either of the present or of the past. This state of ignorance is not due to a lack of capacity to know, but is due to the fact that almost no one has tried to gather those facts of our associated life, which are essential to sound inductions. This could have been done, but it has not been done. The very sad thing about our present predicament is that very few seem to have discovered our gross ignorance. Much that we think we know has no other foundation than the unsupported assertions and opinions of men who perhaps know little more about the real conditions than those who are taught by them. While some sound inductions may be made at the present time, the number is very small comparatively; and the great work of the scientific student of society for some time to come must be the patient gathering of the data of our associated life.

Then are we to burn up all that has been written, and stop writing and talking until we learn something? The writer does not advocate anything so radical as this, but the world wouldn't suffer very much, and certainly the South would be greatly benefited, if much that has been written in histories and other books and periodicals concerning the South, both before and since the war, were consumed in the flames. He does propose, however, that many of "these works" be taken out of the historical and sociological libraries and turned over to the department of pedagogy, psychology, and penology, as most interesting phenomena of childish fancy, mental aberration, and criminal instincts.

It would be unreasonable to demand of those who presume to interpret for us social phenomena that they give us only those facts and inductions which have been established beyond any question. Such a standard is not maintained by any science. But our standard here should be as high as it is in other departments of knowledge —in medicine, for instance. Before a man is given any kind of hearing on the description or diagnosis or treatment of any disorder of the body, he must give unquestioned evidence of both capacity and thorough training in the science of medicine. Certainly

2

we ought to demand as much of those who describe and diagnose and treat the disorders of the social body. From such writers we have a right to demand that they make use of all known facts at hand which are at all germane to the subject discussed; and further that they use reasonable diligence in getting all additional necessary facts which are attainable. From such data many sound and interesting inductions may be made with regard to the conditions in the South, which it would seem have never been made by our voluminous writers. Many additional inductions may be made, and should be made, which are without adequate data at the present time to warrant us in stating them as established. But such inductions must be stated only tentatively; they must not be contradictory to any known fact or principle; and they must be the most reasonable inductions possible from the data at hand.

The writer does not claim to be a historian. But as a student of society he has made some investigations of life in the South, particularly of the period just before the Civil War. He has not, as yet, gone very far with these investigations, but he has gone far enough to convince his own mind, at least, that the real life in the South of this period has not been told, either in our leading histories or in other publications of a similar nature; certainly it is not told in those he has examined.

3. The Conception We Get of Life in the South before the War from the Historians.

1. There was nothing that even remotely approximated Democracy in the South before the Civil War.

2. From the beginning a very small number of large slaveholders were the sole repositories of social, industrial, and political power. There was little or no chance for any poor man, however worthy, to rise in any sphere of life.

3. The aristocrats, who constituted the ruling power in every sphere of life, were proud, arrogant, slothful, dissipated, and lazy.

4. At the bottom of the social organism was a great body of non-slaveholders who composed about seven-tenths of the entire white population. These were illiterate, and they were almost as low as the slaves; their moral condition was groveling baseness. They were the most lazy, the most idle, the most shiftless, the most worthless of men. There were no artisans or mechanics among them, with a few exceptions, and work of every kind they abhorred.

5. The white people of the South of all classes looked down on manual labor.

6. The South was exclusively agricultural, and the Southerners were farming at a great loss. The institution of slavery made the development of manufacturing impossible, and interfered with any development or growth in the Southern States whatsoever.

7. The South paid little attention to education. The Virginians were without Church, university, schools, or literature in any form that required or fostered intellectual life. The great majority of the slaveholders were lacking in ordinary culture. There was no free school system for the whites in the South before the Civil War.

REFERENCES.

Schouler, Vol. II., p. 231; Vol. IV., p. 30; Vol. I., p. 9.
McMaster, Vol. II., p. 14.
Von Holst, Vol. I., pp. 344, 338.
Rhodes, Vol. I., pp. 344-350.
Henry Adams, Vol. I., p. 138.
E. Benjamin Andrews, Vol. II., pp. 4 and 5.
Wilson, Division and Reunion, pp. 105, 106, 127, 128, 104.
Theodore Roosevelt, Winning of the West, Vol. I., p. 130.
W. P. Trent, Life of W. G. Sims, p.
Lyman Abbott, Christianity and Social Problems, p. 38.
The Outlook, March 23, 1901.
Cairnes, Slave Power, Harper's Magazine, Vol. XXIX., p. 123.
Tausig, Tariff History of the United States, p. 73.
Bullock, Introduction to the Study of Economics, p. 27.

To what extent are the conclusions of the historians with reference to conditions in the South in accord with the accessible facts? In the pages that follow an attempt is made to give a partial answer to this question. With this object in view the following subjects are discussed:

I. The Early Population of Virginia and Societary Life in This Colony in the Seventeenth Century.
II. Some Contributions Made by Virginians.
III. Industrial Life in the South.
IV. The Educational Movement in the South before the Civil War.
V. Political Life in Virginia before the Civil War.
VI. The Moral Life of the People from a Study of Crime and Pauperism.
VII. Personal Interviews with Men Who Lived under the Old Régime.

# I. THE EARLY POPULATION OF VIRGINIA AND SOCIETARY LIFE IN THIS COLONY IN THE SEVENTEENTH CENTURY.

It is generally conceded that the white population of Virginia, and of the other Southern States, came originally from the British Isles almost exclusively. Their ancestors were English, Scotch, Scotch-Irish, and Irish.

Southern white people before the Civil War have been divided into two classes by the historians: "The Cavaliers" and the "Poor Whites." By cavaliers they mean descendants of English aristocracy; and by poor whites they mean the descendants of the criminal and semicriminal, the pauper and semipauper classes, whose ancestors came to this country as redemptioners.

## 1. THE VIRGINIA REDEMPTIONER.

"The poor whites [of the South] were made up in great part of the indentured servants whose time had run out. They were the most lazy, the most idle, the most shiftless, the most worthless of men." (McMaster, Vol. II., p. 14.)

### (a) THE COMING OF THE WHITE SERVANTS.

In England in the seventeenth century there was a great oversupply of labor, and in Virginia at the same time there was the greatest demand for labor. In these economic conditions of the two countries was born the idea of the redemptioner—the white servant. The indenture was the means of bringing together across the Atlantic the worker and his work. The poor people of Great Britain who were not able to pay their transportation were allowed to work out the cost of their passage with a Virginia farmer. In addition to these, some who had been convicted of crime in Great Britain were also sent to Virginia as redemptioners. But as a rule these were political criminals—prisoners of war.

Before any reliable conclusions can be reached as to the number and character of the redemptioners that came into the colony of Virginia, the real meaning of certain terms used in this connection must be understood. These terms are "servant," "redemptioner," "criminal," and "Virginia." They had meanings in the colonial days widely different from the meanings they have now. A failure on the part of writers to discover and make this distinction has been the cause of much confusion and misrepresentation with reference to this subject.

## *"Servant."*

The term "servant" did not in those days carry with it the idea of menial work. Neither did it connote the idea of low or obscure birth. It meant nearer what we mean to-day by employee. The attorney of Richard Longman, a merchant of London, is referred to as his servant.

## *"Redemptioner."*

A "redemptioner" was one who redeemed himself, who fulfilled his contract with the planter who paid his expenses across the Atlantic, and thus freed himself from this obligation. The word "redemptioner" carried with it in no sense the idea of crime.

## *"Criminal."*

A "criminal" is one who has violated some law of the government under which he lives. Many—perhaps the very large majority —of the criminals sent to the colonies as redemptioners in the seventeenth century were political criminals. These were simply prisoners of war. George Washington and Patrick Henry would have been placed in this class.

## *"Virginia."*

There is a wide difference between "Virginia" as understood in Great Britain in colonial days and the *Colony* of Virginia. Virginia, as used in England in the seventeenth and eighteenth centuries, meant almost any place on this side of the Atlantic Ocean. It not only included all the American colonies, but included also the West Indies Islands. This confusion continued late in the eighteenth century, perhaps till after the American Revolution.

Then, if we would arrive at the truth with reference to the number and character of redemptioners received by each colony, we must first abandon all conclusions based on the names discussed above, and get back to the real facts behind the names.

REFERENCES.

Records of York County, Va., 1638-1648, p. 356.
Bruce, Economic History of Virginia in the Seventeenth Century, Vol. I., pp. 574, 575, 608, 610, 609.
Fiske, Old Virginia and Her Neighbors, Vol. III., pp. 187, 182, 183, 184.
Records of York County, Va., Vol. 1694-1702, p. 325.
Beverley's History of Virginia, p. 219.
William and Mary College Quarterly, Vol. II., p. 82.
Brown, Genesis of the United States, Vol. II., p. 529. Vol. I., pp. 195, 145, 146.
American Historical Review, Vol. II., pp. 20, 12-19, 21-25, 28, 32.
Henning's Statutes, Vol. II., p. 509.
Sainsbury's Abstracts, p. 117.
A Perfect Description of Virginia, p. 9.
White Servitude in the Colony of Virginia, pp. 25, 35.

(*b*) THE PURPOSE OF ENGLAND IN ESTABLISHING THE COLONY OF VIRGINIA.

The purpose of England in establishing the Colony of Virginia is plainly shown in the strict precautions taken by those who had this work in hand to keep out of this colony all unworthy persons. In "A True and Sincere Declaration of the Purpose and Ends of the Plantation Begun in Virginia," published in 1610, it is announced: "We will receive no man that cannot bring or render some good testimony of his relation to God, and civil manner and behavior to his neighbors with whom he hath lived." There is an abundance of evidence to show that this purpose was strictly adhered to in the early days of this colony.

REFERENCES.

Brown, Genesis of the United States, Vol. I., pp. 296, 353, 355, 361, 362.
Nova Britannia, p. 6.

(*c*) LIFE IN THE COLONY OF VIRGINIA IN THE SEVENTEENTH CENTURY AS TOLD BY CONTEMPORARIES.

From contemporary writers of the seventeenth century, many of whom were or had been citizens of the colony at the time of writing, we get the unqualified statements with reference to the good character of the redemptioners and of the people in general in Virginia at this time.

All the writers here referred to practically agreed. They cover the period of the first one hundred years of the Virginia Colony. They were in close touch with the life of the Virginia Colony at that time, and hence had splendid opportunities to observe the facts. From these writers we draw the following conclusions:

1. The purpose of founding the Colony of Virginia was to establish a permanent, respectable, representative English society on this side of the Atlantic based on the Christian principles of civilization.

2. Criminals, paupers, and other worthless persons were never in demand, and their introduction was always vigorously fought by the colonists.

3. The colonists resented quickly and sharply at all times any insinuations tending to reflect on the character of their population. They claimed that such slanders were gross misrepresentations, and had no basis whatever in fact.

4. The great body of the redemptioners were honest, hard-working men, and had nothing in common with criminals and paupers. The work they did was the same kind of work done by all the colonists. Honest toil was honored by all, and was followed by all. The redemptioner had the respect of the whole community. He was amply protected by the laws of the colony while he was under contract, and was received in every way as an equal when his term of service closed.

5. All redemptioners had the same rights and privileges, and no mention is made of any who had been criminals.

6. The character of the life of the community, as described by these writers, is totally inconsistent with the idea that a large number of the criminal and pauper classes had been brought into the colony. The people were unusually honest, and the inclination to accept charity was most remarkably weak. These two characteristics are found to-day only among self-respecting, honest, and industrious people.

7. Society was very democratic. Almost no one was in need, and few could be called rich. The best places in the gift of the people were open to all, and redemptioners rose to positions of honor and trust. There is not the slightest evidence of a ruling aristocracy or of a degraded multitude.

8. If criminals and paupers were sent to Virginia in any considerable number in the seventeenth century, these writers seem to have been entirely ignorant of the fact.

9. The redemptioners most in demand in the Virginia Colony were young boys about sixteen years of age.

REFERENCES.

A True Declaration of the State of the Colony in Virginia, pp. 3-5.
New Life in Virginia, p. 13.
Brown, Genesis of the United States, Vol. I., p. 592; Vol. II., p. 798.
Bruce, Economic History of Virginia, etc., Vol. I., p. 592.
American Historical Review, Vol. II., p. 23.
A Perfect Description of Virginia, pp. 3, 6, 7, 8.
Bullock's History of Virginia, p. 53.
Leah and Rachel, pp. 2, 11, 12, 15, 16, 17, 19.
Beverley's History of Virginia, pp. 219, 220, 223.

(d) CORROBORATING FACTS FROM THE RECORDS.

There is overwhelming proof that boys were in most demand in Virginia as redemptioners. So great was this demand that kidnaping, stealing, gross misrepresentations and almost every other conceivable method was resorted to by the shipmasters to secure children for the plantations. The evil became so alarming in England that Parliament fixed the death penalty for child-stealing.

The census of the Colony of Virginia for 1624-25 shows the youthful character of the redemptioners. The ages of eighty-six redemptioners are here given—their ages when they arrived in the colony—and there is no reason that these should not be taken as thoroughly representative of the ages of all the redemptioners in the colony at that time. They may be classified as follows:

Sixteen years old and younger (nearly one-half)......................... 34
Twenty-one years old and younger (all except sixteen)................... 70
Number over twenty-five years of age................................... 4

In 1670 Virginia passed a law prohibiting the importation of any redemptioner who had been convicted of crime of any kind. Even political criminals were prohibited from coming into the colony. This law was approved by the king, and there is the strongest evidence that it was rigidly enforced.

The redemptioners were protected by the laws of the colony

against any kind of harsh treatment at the hands of the masters, and were given every right and privilege possible while under indenture. When they had served their apprenticeship, they were given all the rights and privileges of citizenship that were possessed by the leading men of the colony. There is nothing in the treatment they received to indicate that any of them were criminals. There is everything to show that they were regarded as honest, worthy people. A number of the redemptioners rose to places of honor and trust.

REFERENCES.

A Perfect Description of Virginia, p. 3.
Sainsbury's Abstracts, pp. 3, 54, 58, 59, 60, 74, 117.
English MSS., Part I., Appendix to Fourth Report, p. 232.
Virginia Carrolum, pp. 14, 16, 21, 23, 39, 40, 42, 81, 82, 279, 261.
Bruce, Economic History of Virginia, etc., Vol. I., pp. 612, 608, 605; Vol. II., p. 611.
Henning's Statutes, Vol. II., pp. 509, 117, 165, 135; Vol. III., pp. 447-452, 435; Vol. I., pp. 156, 257, 43, 388.
Ballaugh, p. 35.
American Historical Review, Vol. II., p. 16.
Fiske, Old Virginia and Her Neighbors, Vol. II., p. 184.
Virginia's Cure, p. 16.
Virginia Carrolum, pp. 290, 399.
Ballaugh, White Servitude, p. 371.

(*e*) THE NUMBER AND CHARACTER OF THE REDEMPTIONERS WHO WERE SENT TO THE OTHER AMERICAN COLONIES.

To get an idea of the number of redemptioners that went to the other American colonies, and the number of criminals accepted by these colonies, we must first get their attitude to this class of immigrants. The shipmaster would naturally carry the redemptioners to the particular colony in which the demand was greatest for this class of labor, and where the opposition to redemptioners with questionable characters was least.

### New York.

The Colony of New York was not only not hostile to the importation of convicts as redemptioners, but as late as 1693 put forth special efforts to have this class of people brought into the colony.

## Pennsylvania.

The first protest that came from Pennsylvania against the importation into the colony of persons guilty of heinous crimes was not till 1722. This protest was very mild. Pennsylvania simply wanted to put a tariff on heinous criminals coming into the colony.

## Rhode Island.

In 1714, bringing in an Indian as a servant or slave was prohibited under a penalty of fifty pounds. The reason given for this law was that such importations "daily discouraged the importation of white servants from Great Britain." Certainly the demand of Rhode Island for redemptioners was very great at this time, and we hear of no protest whatever from this colony against redemptioners who had been convicted of crime.

## Massachusetts.

That the people of Massachusetts began to buy white servants soon after they arrived in America, there is no question. Although redemptioners had been coming into the Colony of Massachusetts for a half century, and among them certainly many political criminals, no law was passed and no protest was made with reference to criminal redemptioners by this colony before the close of the seventeenth century. The first time the question was taken up at all by the Colony of Massachusetts was in 1700. This was thirty years after the Colony of Virginia had prohibited by statutes the bringing in of any redemptioners who had been convicted of crime of any kind. The law passed in 1700, which John Fiske characterizes as "stringent laws against bringing in convicts," makes no mention of redemptioners whatever; it can apply to them only by inference. There is nothing in this law that even indicates that Massachusetts either prohibited or was opposed to the bringing in of those who had been convicted of crime. There was a law, however, passed in 1709 in Massachusetts which bears directly on the question of the importation of redemptioners, and which is very explicit. This law was as follows: "In 1709 the General Court of Massachusetts offered a bounty of forty shillings to any one who would bring in and dispose in service—that is, sell into bondage more or less lasting—*any white male between the ages of eight and twenty-five years."* The bounty of Massachusetts was equal to nearly one-fourth of the total cost of the redemptioner to the shipmaster.

Then in the early part of the eighteenth century there was a very extraordinary demand in New England for redemptioners, and large bounties were offered for their introduction. In New York the demand was so great that the colony in 1692, in an official capacity, petitioned for the "felons" in Newgate to be sent into their midst. When the demand was so great for redemptioners in New England and New York, we find Virginia, in 1699, laying a tax of $17 on the importation of all servants not born in England or Wales.

The fact that the demand for redemptioners was much greater in the New England colonies and in New York in the early part of the eighteenth century than it was in Virginia is easily established. The reasons for this are very plain to those who look under the surface and really want to know the truth.

The great importation of convicts into the American colonies was after 1717, or between 1717 and the American Revolution. The number of convicts sent to the American colonies after 1717 can only be approximated. It is estimated that not less than ten thousand convicts from the "Old Bailey" prison alone were sent to the colonies between 1717 and 1775. Where did these convicts land?

The opposition in Virginia to the bringing in of redemptioners who had been convicted of crime, which finally culminated in the sweeping law of 1670, was largely moral. This act on the part of the Virginians was against their immediate economic interests. At this time there were but 2,000 negro slaves in the colony, and the colonists were still dependent on the redemptioners for labor. But about this time the Virginians discovered that slave labor was more profitable to them than white labor under indenture. So they began to substitute slave labor in place of that of the redemptioners long before the great importation of convicts to the American colonies. In proof of the substitution of the slaves for the redemptioner, we find that there was a very rapid increase in the slave population after 1670 and a relative decrease in the white population.

PERCENTAGE INCREASE IN POPULATION IN VIRGINIA.

| White Population. | Per Cent. | Slave Population. | Per Cent. |
|---|---|---|---|
| From 1634 to 1649 (14 years)... | 203 | From 1671 to 1700.............. | 200 |
| From 1649 to 1671 (22 years)... | 153 | From 1700 to 1715.............. | 283 |
| From 1671 to 1700 (29 years)... | 55 | | |
| From 1700 to 1715 (15 years)... | 20 | From 1715 to 1763............. | 552 |
| From 1715 to 1763 (48 years)... | 94 | | |

If the contention is well-grounded that the Northern colonies received a much larger per cent of the redemptioners who came in the eighteenth century, we should expect to find a larger increase in the white population of these colonies than in Virginia, and this we do find.

PERCENTAGE INCREASE IN WHITE POPULATION.

| | Virginia. | Mass. | Pa. & Del. | New Jersey. | Conn. |
|---|---|---|---|---|---|
| From 1700 to 1715.......... | 20 | 34 | 116 | 110 | ... |
| From 1700 to 1750.......... | 116 | 185 | 825 | 700 | ... |
| From 1715 to 1750.......... | 72 | 108 | 329 | 428 | 139 |

In view of all these facts, with New York petitioning for convicts and Massachusetts offering large bounties for white male servants, we are driven to the conclusion that the large majority of the thousands of convicts sent over to America in the eighteenth century must have gone to the Northern colonies. If Virginia prohibited such immigrants coming in when white labor was almost the sole dependence of the colony and was in great demand, there is no reason for thinking that the colony accepted them when the demands for labor had been satisfied by the slaves.

CONCLUSION.

1. It is probable that Virginia received very few redemptioners in the seventeenth and eighteenth centuries who had been convicted of crime in England.

2. Of the relatively small number of criminals who came into this colony, it is probable that the large majority of them had been convicted of some political offense only.

3. It is highly probable that Virginia received a much smaller number of redemptioners who had been convicted of crime, in pro-

portion to her population, than was received by many of the Northern colonies.

REFERENCES.

American Historical Review, Vol. II., pp. 22, 23, 21, 24, 20, 32, 25.
Holland Documents, 1603-1656, Vol. I., p. 99.
Documents Relating to Colonial History of New York, Vol. XIV., p. 31.
Massachusetts Acts and Resolves, Vol. II., p. 634 (quoted by Prof. Butler).
Henning's Statutes, Vol. III., p. 193; Vol. II., pp. 510, 516.
Fiske, Old Virginia and Her Neighbors, Vol. II., pp. 193, 191.
Bullock, History of Virginia, p. 39.
Ballaugh, White Servitude, pp. 37, 38.
McDonald Papers, Vol. XVI., p. 155; Vol. II., p. 21.
Bruce, Economic History of Virginia, Vol. II., p. 319.
Virginia Carrolum, pp. 114, 115.
A Perfect Description of Virginia, p. 3.
Cook, History of Virginia, p. 109.
Thwaite, pp. 265, 266.

## 2. THE CAVALIER.

"The immigrants to Virginia and the South, sons of the Cavalier, looked down upon industry as their fathers had done before them." (Lyman Abbott, Christianity and Social Problems, p. 165.)

"The political system of the South was an oligarchy. Less than 8,000 planters in the South were the true center of this oligarchy." (Rhodes, Vol. I., p. 344.)

"Virginia was colonized by gentlemen, and often helpless ones at that; blood and pedigree always ruled in Virginia." (Schouler, Vol. I., p. 9; Vol. II., p. 231.)

### (a) CAVALIERS AND ROUNDHEADS IN ENGLAND.

Of all the terms used by superficial historians to misrepresent the facts of Southern history, there is but one, perhaps, that has done a larger service in this unholy work than "Virginia Redemptioner," and that term is "Virginia" or "Southern Cavalier." In England, Cavaliers and Roundheads were the names of opposing political parties in the seventeenth century. The name "Cavalier" was applied to those who supported Charles I., and the name "Roundhead" to those who followed Cromwell. The difference between these two parties was primarily a political difference. On the one side was Charles I., incompetent, tyrannical, and wicked, but in large measure true to the traditions of the English people, and standing for the established order of things. On the other side were Cromwell and his coadjutors, radical, tyrannical, and thoroughly imbued with fanaticism.

The fact that an Englishman supported Charles I. gave no indication whatever of his real sympathies with reference to democracy and aristocracy. If Mr. Gladstone, England's greatest democrat, had lived in the time of Charles the First, we have every reason to believe that he would have been found among the Cavaliers. That there were many tyrants among the Cavaliers, it is quite certain; but the number, in all probability, was no greater than the number of such people found in the ranks of the Roundheads.

(*b*) THE COMING OF THE CAVALIERS TO AMERICA.

All agree that the period of the coming of the Cavalier to America was the period of the Commonwealth in England. The time, then, was from 1649 to 1660. It is also admitted that Tide Water Virginia was the section of this country in which all the Cavaliers settled.

The only reliable evidence as to the actual coming of the Cavalier the writer has been able to find is that given by Robert Beverly in his history of Virginia, and this is not very definite. The second revised edition of Mr. Beverly's history was printed in 1722. Mr. Beverly said: "In the time of the rebellion in England *several* good Cavalier families went thither [to Virginia] with their affects." Nothing whatever is said of the character of these Cavaliers except that they were "good Cavalier families." Mr. Beverly was a native Virginian, and perhaps remembered the time of the coming of the Cavaliers. Virginia had but a small population then, and all the people lived in the few counties in the Tide Water section. In such a small section, with such a small population, it was very easy to estimate the number of any particular class of immigrants with great accuracy.

Mr. Fiske, in "Old Virginia and Her Neighbors," makes no reference to Beverly's estimate; but he tries hard to establish the fact that Beverly was wrong, and that a considerable number of Cavaliers came to Virginia at this time. In support of his position Mr. Fiske makes three arguments. The first argument made is that the great Cavalier exodus from England must have been a chief cause of the remarkable increase of the white population of Virginia from 15,000 in 1649 to 38,000 in 1670. But the percentage of increase in population for the fourteen years preceding the coming of the Cavalier was 205 per cent; the percentage increase in population for the fourteen years after the first coming of the Cavalier was 80 per cent. The next argument advanced by Mr. Fiske in support of his theory is the fact that there was a marked increase in the size of land grants from 1649 to 1660. But, as a matter of fact, the number of land grants containing 5,000 acres and over was as large in proportion to population in 1634 as in the whole period of five years (1651-55) after the coming of the Cavalier. The average number of acres in a grant was greater in 1634 and in 1643 than in the period from 1651 to 1655. The number of acres in a single tract, the average number of acres in a grant, and the number of grants exceeding 5,000 acres were greater after the period of the coming of the Cavalier than during this period. The last argument given by Mr. Fiske is as follows: "It is in the reign of Charles II. that the student of Virginia history begins to meet frequently with the familiar names, such as Randolph, Pendleton, Madison, Mason, Monroe, Cary, Ludwell, Parke, Robinson, Marshall, Washington, and so many others that have become eminent. All these were Cavalier families that came to Virginia after the downfall of Charles I." The writer has access to only a small number of the names of those who came over to Virginia before 1649, but in this very small list he finds that three of the eleven named by Mr. Fiske were in Virginia long before 1649. If Mr. Fiske were correct in his statement of facts, it would be reckless in the extreme to draw any inference whatever as to family connections in England on a basis of names alone. In this way Jack Monroe, minor prize fighter, could be shown to be a direct descendant of President James Monroe, and Booker Washington a direct descendant of George Washington. To show how unreliable such evidence is, we have a list of thirty-two felons sent out from the "Old Bailey" prison in 1731 to some of the English plantations. In this list of English felons we find the names of one of our Presidents, the names of Cabinet officers, United States Senators, Governors, university professors, prominent ministers, etc.

But suppose Mr. Fiske is right in his contention that there was a great influx of Cavaliers between 1649 and 1660, there is nothing whatever to show that these men were proud, aristocratic, tyrannical, and haughty, or that they had any of those characteristics which were attributed to the extreme Cavaliers in England. On the other hand, every fact obtainable with reference to the life of the colony after the arrival of these good Cavalier families shows that there could not have been any considerable number of proud, haughty, aristocratic men in Virginia at this time. All the facts go to show that life in the colony was very democratic, and that all of the citizens stood on an equal footing.

(*c*) POLITICAL LIFE IN VIRGINIA AFTER THE COMING OF THE
CAVALIER.

In 1655-56 the General Assembly of Virginia passed the following suffrage law: "Whereas we conceive it something hard and unagreeable to reason that any person should pay equal taxes and yet have no vote in elections, therefore it is enacted by the present Grand Assembly that so much of the act for choosing burgesses be repealed as excludes freemen from votes." This was six years after the first coming of the Cavaliers. Universal manhood suffrage continued in Virginia for fifteen years. In 1670, on account of the fact that certain worthless people made great tumults at the elections, suffrage was restricted to freeholders and housekeepers. But the restriction was very slight, since land was so cheap that any one could become a landholder with practically no effort, and almost every man was a housekeeper in those days. But, slight as this restriction was, it was swept away six years later. But through the mandate of the king and the influence of Berkeley a law was enacted that freeholders only were to be electors. This law came not from the Colony of Virginia.

The highest offices in the gift of the people were open to every white man in the colony, and it was very common for men who came over as redemptioners to be elected to the highest offices in the gift of the people after the coming of the Cavalier.

In these facts we can find no evidence of the existence of a tyrannical oligarchy. There is not a single fact that indicates any kind of aristocratic influence shaping the life of the colony at this time. On the other hand, it is very clear that there was no thought of a privileged class. Every man in public life stood on his own merits alone.

To fully understand and appreciate the intensely democratic and liberal spirit back of the suffrage laws of Virginia for this period, one must remember that this experiment in democracy was new. Virginia had no precedent, either in England or New England, for this radical departure. In England the suffrage was strictly limited to freeholders. In New England the restrictions were much greater. Massachusetts during this period was ruled by a small ecclesiastical oligarchy, and the right of suffrage was denied to at least three-fourths of the freemen of that colony. Citizenship was given only to those who were members of the Congregational Church. Business shrewdness, no less than religious exclusiveness, dictated these regulations. The germ of Massachusetts citizenship at this period is not to be found in conscience but in the freedom of a trading company. The ecclesiastical test of citizenship seems to have been an afterthought. Class lines in Massachusetts were closely drawn. The "gentry" was distinguished from the "generality." It was for the "gentry" that the "assistant" positions were invariably reserved. The "assistants" in Massachusetts corresponded in a general way to the burgesses in Virginia. From the pulpit the doctrine was preached that the "assistant's" right to his office was as inviolable as that of the private citizen to his freehold.

For sixty years Massachusetts maintained the right of the few to rule without any reference whatever to the wishes of three-fourths of her adult male population. In this period no progress whatever was made toward greater liberality in conferring the right of citizenship. The emancipation came in 1691, but it came not from Massachusetts; it came from the king of England over the most stubborn and the most persistent protests of this oligarchy. In Massachusetts the English sovereign interceded in the interests of democracy, demanding that the right of citizenship should be given to all worthy persons on the basis of a reasonable qualification. In Virginia, long after the coming of the Cavalier, the English sovereign interceded also, but here it was to put a check on democracy.

(*d*) THE DISTRIBUTION OF WEALTH IN VIRGINIA IN THE SEVEN-
TEENTH CENTURY.

From a list of the estates appraised in York and in other representative counties in Virginia in the latter part of the seventeenth

3

century, it is very clear that there were but few rich men in the colony at the beginning of the eighteenth century. Perhaps there were none who would be considered rich to-day. The distribution of wealth was very democratic, and the differences in the value of the estates were such as we should expect to find in any democratic farming community. There is nothing here that points to the existence of any wealthy aristocratic class.

There was very little luxury in the colony at this time. The people, with very few exceptions, seemed to have lived in great simplicity. "The typical dwelling of Virginia in the seventeenth century (and innumerable examples of the same kind have survived to the present day) was a frame building of moderate size with a chimney at each end."

#### (e) THE INTEREST OF THE COLONY IN EDUCATION.

An endowed free school was established in Virginia in or before 1649. This was perhaps the first free school established in America.

In 1661-62 the Assembly at Jamestown passed the following act: "Be it enacted that, for the advancement of learning, education of youth, supply of the ministry, and promotion of piety, there be land taken up for a college and *free school*." In Beverly's "History of Virginia," the second revised edition of which was printed in London in 1722, we have the following: "There are large tracts of land, houses, and other things granted to free schools for the education of children in many parts of the country [Virginia] ; and some of these are so large that in themselves they are a handsome maintainance to a master."

#### CONCLUSION.

From this study of the population of Virginia in the seventeenth century the following general conclusions may be drawn:

1. Virginia, on account of unusual precautions and on account of her peculiar economic conditions, in all probability received a smaller number of redemptioners who had been convicted of crime, in proportion to her population, than almost any of the other American colonies.

2. The theory that a large number of rich, aristocratic, extreme Cavaliers came over in 1649 and monopolized all industrial and

political powers first in Virginia and later in other Southern colonies is totally without foundation. There is no evidence that any such people, in numbers worth considering, came to Virginia at all; and the character of the life in the colony after they are said to have come contradicts such a theory at every point.

3. There was no leisure class in Virginia at this time.

4. Class distinctions counted for nothing in the public life of the colony.

5. Life was very simple and very democratic, and merit alone counted in the struggle for preferment.

6. If there were ever a tyrannical oligarchy in Virginia, we can find no evidence of it in the seventeenth century.

REFERENCES.

Fiske, Old Virginia, etc., Vol. II., pp. 12, 16, 24, 25, 5.
Beverley, History of Virginia, pp. 232, 224.
Virginia Carrolum, pp. 114, 329.
Leah and Rachel, p. 17.
Brown, Genesis of the United States, Vol. I., p. 281; Vol. II., pp. 940, 983.
American Historical Review, Vol. II., p. 31.
Bishop Meades, Old Churches and Families of Virginia, Vol. II., p. 97.
Henning's Statutes, Vol. I., p. 403; Vol. II., pp. 425, 280, 356; Vol. I., p. 475; Vol. III., pp. 26, 173.
Virginia's Cure, p. 16.
J. H. U. S., Vol. XII., pp. 279, 386, 394, 396, 385, 422, 426, 429, 393, 453.
Records of York County, in Virginia State Library.
Records of Hanover County, Hanover Courthouse.
Bruce, Economic History, etc., Vol. II., pp. 151-154, 247-254.
Thorpe, Constitutional History, etc., Vol. I., p. 192.

# II. SOME CONTRIBUTIONS MADE BY VIRGINIA.

—

We are told by the historians that this progressive democratic community, which promised so much for civilization at the close of the seventeenth century, within the lifetime of many who were living at that time was transformed into an aristocracy, the most tyrannical and the most degrading that has ever been known in a civilized community. History nowhere else gives an account of such social and individual degeneration among a people once civilized as is recorded with reference to the white people of Virginia and of the other Southern States in the eighteenth and nineteenth centuries. This small slaveholding aristocracy, we are told, had all political, social, and industrial power, and ruled with an iron hand. They lived in idleness and luxury and dissipation, and were unmerciful in their treatment of the great masses of their fellow-citizens who were of their own blood. They drove them from all the soil that was fertile, gave them no recognition of any kind, denied them any opportunity to rise, forced them into a state little above that of the slave, and made them the mudsill of a most degenerate society.

### Some of the Men Produced by This Degenerate Society.

In the General Assembly of Virginia on the eve of the American Revolution we find a man who was neither an aristocrat in property nor in blood. At this time the American colonies were face to face with one of the world's greatest crises, and they needed a man. At this critical moment in the Virginia Assembly this representative from the masses rose, and with invincible courage and matchless eloquence sent an electric thrill throughout the land. Under the influence of this great orator and patriot, men hesitated no longer; they cast their fears to the winds, and shouldered their muskets in defense of their rights. But what did Patrick Henry know of liberty?

Two years later the colonists found themselves face to face with another crisis. Up to this time they had been fighting not for independence but for their rights as Englishmen. Now, it was felt that any further efforts in this direction would be futile. The general feeling was that the colonies must either unconditionally submit or declare their independence. But they were Englishmen and Scotchmen, and this was revolution. Naturally they hesitated a long time to take a step so radical. Finally, Congress met and appointed a committee of five to draft a declaration of independence. On this committee was New England's favorite son, John Adams; but John Adams did not write the Declaration of Independence. On this committee was also a young Virginian whose father was a commoner, and it was from his brain and heart the great document came. Every word of this document throbbed with liberty and brotherhood. It seemed more than a human production; it almost carried with it the credentials of divine inspiration. But what did this man know of human rights?

After the independence of the colonies was declared, they needed a man of action. The precarious conditions demanded a man who could do the seemingly impossible. Again, the splendid environments of New England and of the other Northern colonies were passed over, and they came to this "Gehenna" to find a commander in chief of the army of the Revolution.

But not only did Virginia furnish the leaders of the Revolution, but she also sent to the front more than her *pro rata* of those who stood on the firing line and endured the hardships of an awful war. "The white male population of Virginia and Pennsylvania over sixteen years of age was about the same, yet 56,000 Virginians went to the front when but 34,000 Pennsylvanians. New York had double the military population of South Carolina, while New Hampshire was slightly greater. Yet from this small State the Southerners who shouldered muskets outnumbered the New Hampshire men more than two to one, and they exceeded New York's quota by 29,000. In South Carolina thirty-seven Southerners out of every forty-two were able to enlist and fight, and they did so."

That such loyalty and patriotism and self-sacrifice and *seeming* love of liberty and courage should have been shown by this degraded population of Virginia and of the other Southern States in the Revolution is one of the strange things that no man has explained.

Concerning the part the Old Dominion played in the constructive work of this government we will let Mr. John Fiske speak: "In the work of constructing our National Government and putting it into operation there were five men distinguished above all others. In an especial sense they deserved to be called the five founders of the American Union. Naming them chronologically in the order of the time at which the influence of each was most powerfully felt, they came as follows: George Washington, James Madison, Alexander Hamilton, Thomas Jefferson, and John Marshall."

The known facts of the life and ancestry of Washington, Jefferson, Henry, Madison, Marshall, and Monroe do not indicate that a single one of these men was a descendant of English aristocracy, or that either one was reared in luxury. In the lives of these men, who molded and shaped the public life of Virginia for more than a half century, we fail to find a single autocratic, tyrannical characteristic, which the historians tell us characterized all the Southern leaders before the war.

Of the first thirty-six years of the life of the republic, thirty-two of these were passed with Virginians in the White House; and each of the four distinguished men elected to the Presidency from Virginia in this period was honored with a second term. While five Southern men were honored with reëlection to the Presidency before 1860, covering a period of forty years, not a single President from any other section of this country ever received this honor before the Civil War.

No nation, however great, within the short period of three-fourths of a century can be expected to furnish but a very small number of world characters. Some great people go for centuries without producing any men whose real greatness takes them beyond the bounds of their own country. In the "World's Hall of Fame" there are yet many vacant places, and still the building is small. How many Americans at the close of the Civil War had won and deserved a place in this temple, and where were they from?

Would not an unbiased judge give the first places in America as follows: In statesmanship, Washington; in philosophy, Madison or Jefferson; in law, Marshall; in military art, Lee; in oratory, Henry; in poetry, Poe?

Not only were the great leaders in the South blind to the awful facts so well understood by the historians, but these facts were also hidden from the eyes of all the rest of the Southerners. All believed they were living under a democracy; all believed they were enjoying the inalienable rights of life, liberty, and the pursuit of happiness; all believed that they were free, and were living under governments that gave equal rights to all and special privileges to none. So strongly were they convinced that these things were true that they were willing to surrender their lives in defense of the order under which they lived. The first intimation that Southern society was totally depraved, that it was built on injustice and was destructive of life and liberty, came from the Northern historians.

# III. INDUSTRIAL LIFE IN THE SOUTH.

"The system [slavery] produced one of the most singular non-productive classes that any country has ever seen." (Woodrow Wilson, "Division and Reunion," p. 106.)

How the aristocracy obtained and retained its absolute power over the great masses of the people in the South should have been explained by the historians. But, strange to say, they nowhere even attempt an explanation. The answer to this question, and the only answer that has been given, is that this power was obtained through the institution of African slavery. How the institution of slavery proved such a powerful and such a successful means in bringing about this state of things, no one has explained nor attempted to explain at all adequately.

The Virginia Colony had been organized and had been growing rapidly for nearly a century before African slavery became a factor in the life of the colony. The people were here, and the most of them had been here a long time, and the industrial, social, and political foundation of the colony had been thoroughly established long before the slaves in any considerable number had been imported. At the beginning of the eighteenth century, when the slaves began to come in more rapidly, there were no men of great wealth in the colony as far as we are able to learn, and the distribution of wealth was very democratic. Any kind of a capitalistic monopoly under such conditions, of course, would have been impossible; and certainly no one possessed a legal monopoly on slaves.

These African slaves were brought into Virginia by the New England slave dealers and sold at the highest market price. The market price for slaves was fixed by the great law of supply and demand, which fixes the price of everything sold in open market where competition is free. Slaves were sold to anybody who was able to pay the market price, just as horses and machinery were taken into Massachusetts and sold to any one who would pay the market price. It was no more possible or feasible for a few men in Virginia to buy up all the slaves and drive the great masses out of the market than it was for a few men in Massachusetts or New York to buy up all the horses and other means of production and drive the great masses in those sections out of the market. This was not only true in the first purchase of slaves, but it was true of the sale and ownership of slaves in every case down to the time of the emancipation. Slaves were always on the market, and were always sold to the highest bidder without any regard whatever to the heredity or to the social or any other kind of standing of the purchaser; and they were always sold for what they were worth, just as wheat and corn and pork were sold for their market value. In Virginia and all over the South where land was cheap and fertile it was in the power of every industrious man to become a slave owner.

From the census reports of 1860 we get the following: Total number of slaveholders in all the Southern States, 383,637; total number of slaves in the South in 1860, 3,948,713; the average number of slaves to each owner, 10. Only about one-fourth of Southern men owned any slaves at all, one-fifth of the slaveholders owned only one slave, and more than half of the slaveholders owned less than five. There were but 2,293 men in all the Southern States that owned more than 100 slaves. There were but 312 men in all the Southern States that owned more than 200 slaves, and only fourteen owned more than 500 slaves. The number of slaves here given included the whole slave population—the men, the women, the children, the old, the maimed, the halt, the blind.

### I. SLAVE MONOPOLY.

To what extent did large slave ownership give a differential advantage over the farmer who owned a small number of slaves or who owned no slaves at all? The large factory, we know, by virtue of its largeness has such a differential advantage over the small factory at the present time that the small factories, for the most part, have been driven out of business, and the owners in many cases have been driven to financial ruin. Agriculture is very different from manufacturing in this particular. In agriculture, and especially where little machinery is used, as was the case in the South before the war, the large farmer has no differential advantage whatever over the small farmer. On the other hand, the reverse is often true.

Then if there was a slave oligarchy or a slave monopoly in the South before the Civil War, and not a horse oligarchy or a sheep oligarchy or a factory oligarchy in the North, this state of things had no foundation whatever in economic laws. But the facts as recorded in the census reports show conclusively that no ʻsuch monopoly was in existence.

## 2. LAND MONOPOLY.

"The poor whites were driven off the fertile land by the encroachments of the planters or were prevented from occupying the verdant soil by the outbidding of the wealthy." (Rhodes, Vol. I., p. 344.)

"His power as a landed and slave proprietor drove out the small yeomen, cowed the tradesman and the mechanic, and deprived the South of a thrifty middle class." (W. P. Trent, "Life of W. G. Simms," p. 39.)

Monopoly in agricultural lands is possible only where the supply of land is very limited, and where there are many immense fortunes. But in the South good land was almost unlimited in supply, and was always cheap; and in all the Southern States there was perhaps not a single man whose fortune was equal to the fortunes of those considered only in moderate circumstances to-day in the cities of New York, Chicago, and Boston. In Virginia there were only eight men who owned between 200 and 300 slaves, and only one man that owned more than 300 slaves, and this man owned less than 400 slaves. George Vanderbilt has spent more on his home in North Carolina than the combined wealth of all the big slave owners in Virginia in 1860.

Good land was always for sale, and it sold for what it was worth, no more and no less, just as land is sold on the market to-day. The price then, as to-day, was fixed by the law of supply and demand. Good land was never higher in the South than it was in the North; in fact, it was not so high, for there was more good land in proportion to the population in the South than in the North. The opportunities for the few to get control of the good land was certainly much greater in New England, where the supply of fertile lands was very limited, than in Virginia and in the other Southern States, where there was practically no limit to the supply of productive land. There is a sufficient amount of space, and a sufficient amount of productive land, in the one State of Texas to support every man, woman, and child in the South to-day; and Texas is no larger to-day than it was before the Civil War.

Any one should know that the same laws governed land owner-ship in Virginia and in all the other Southern States before the Civil War that were in operation in the agricultural regions of New York, Pennsylvania, Ohio, and Illinois; and the relative position and the relative opportunity of the poor man to the rich man were exactly the same in the one section as in the other, as far as land ownership was concerned. As a matter of fact, the large farmers of the Northern States had a much better opportunity to monopolize the productive lands in their respective communities than were possessed by the large farmers of equal wealth in the Southern States. In the South a very large part of the capital of each slave-holder was invested in slaves, in labor; whereas the amount of the capital expended for labor or invested in labor in the North was relatively small. This gave the Northern farmer an opportunity to invest a larger proportion of his capital in land than was feasible or possible for the slave owner. But land monopoly was unknown and impossible in both sections.

When the census reports of 1860 are examined, no basis whatever is found for land monopoly in the South. These reports indicate that the relative position of the poor man with reference to land ownership was certainly as favorable in the South as in any other section of this country. In fact, the small farmer of the South seems to have held a better relative position in this particular than was held by the small farmer of the North.

*Farms Containing from Three to Five Hundred Acres.*

New England States, one to every seventeen and three-tenths of free population.

Southern States, one to every twelve and one-tenth of free population.

Remaining States, one to every fourteen and nine-tenths of free population.

### 3. THE RELATIVE ADVANTAGE IN SLAVE OWNERSHIP.

Did slave ownership give any special economic advantage? Long before there was any moral sentiment against the institution of slavery the Northern people brought their slaves South and sold them, because they were convinced that the money they had invested in slaves would be more profitable to them invested in some other kind of property.

The general assumption seems to be that if a man owned a number of slaves he could quit work, live in leisure and idleness, have plenty of money to spend and waste, and still hold his property intact; whereas if a man owned property of an equal value in other investments, all admit that he was compelled to be diligent and careful in looking after his business, otherwise he was in great danger of losing his property. There is not the first element of truth, reason, or common sense in this assumption as to the peculiar advantages of slave property. (Slave labor was just as expensive in the South before the war as free labor would have been under similar economic conditions. Slaves were bought and sold in the open market, where competition was free; and under such conditions of course every slave sold for what he was worth, just as the free workingman of the North sold his labor for what it was worth. The only financial difference between slave labor and free labor was that the slave owner made an estimate of what the slave would be worth to him for a life period, both in production and in *reproduction*, just as a man makes an estimate of the value of a cow that he buys; and then, after deducting a sufficient amount for the risk of sickness and early death, and for the yearly expenses of keeping the slaves, he paid the price—the market price, the true value— as far as it could be fixed; whereas in free labor the estimate was made for one year or one month or one day instead of for life. In both cases the market value was paid for the labor, and neither party had any advantage over the other.

1. The slave owner had to look after every interest of the slave— his food, his clothing, his shelter, his health, his habits, his discipline. No one of these could be neglected. The man who worked free, intelligent white labor was relieved from all this.

2. In case of unusually low prices, or in case of industrial depression or drought, the farmer who worked free labor could with great ease curtail his expenses by reducing the amount of his labor and thus save himself from any serious loss; whereas the slaveholder was practically helpless under such adverse conditions. He

could not sell his slaves at such time without great loss, and it was impossible for him to reduce his expenses.

3. The worker of free white labor, with little trouble or expense, could take advantage of changed conditions, new demands, increased demands in certain fields, either by training his employees, which was easy with intelligent, ambitious white men, or by replacing them with others already trained in the new field. The slaveholder was greatly handicapped in this; he could not exchange his workers, and to train the negro slaves for new fields of employment with profit was practically impossible.

4. The man who worked free labor could trust his employees to look after his interests and to do honest work in a way that was impossible to the slaveholder.

Instead of slave-ownership enabling the owner to live in idleness ånd luxury and abundance, greater industry and diligence and careful business management were required of him than were required of the man who worked free labor; and the slaveholder was always in greater danger of a more serious loss than the man who worked free labor. The fact that hundreds of thousands of free white men were employed in the South before 1860 and received as high wages as farm hands received in the North shows that there was no special advantage in slave labor.

4. THE ATTITUDE OF THE WHITE PEOPLE OF THE SOUTH TO MANUAL LABOR.

"Here [in the South] the instinct to keep up the gentleman in social life scorned retail trade and all honest livelihood by manual labor; habits of idle dissipation were common to whites of every grade." (Schouler, Vol. IV., p. 30.)

"Work of every kind they [the poor whites] abhorred. For men who made their living as mechanics, etc., the poor whites felt a contempt." (McMaster, Vol. II., p. 14.)

"The demoralizing influence of the scorn entertained for labor showed itself especially 'upon these [the poor whites]." (Von Holst, Vol. I., p. 344.)

"The system produced one of the most singular nonproductive classes that any country has ever seen. This was the class known in the South as the poor whites." (Woodrow Wilson, D. and R., pp. 105, 128.)

People may be divided into two great classes—those who work and those who do not. The workers may then be divided into two classes—those who do serviceable work, and those whose work is destructive. Then the useful workers of the world may be subdivided into three classes—those who work with their hands, those who work with their brains, and those who work with their hearts.

In the broad and only true sense that work should be considered there was no idle class in the South before the Civil War. The great majority of the white people of the South, as is true of every section, were not fitted for the higher work—the work of the brain and of the heart. Their proper sphere was the sphere of manual labor. But we are told by the historians that they refused to do manual labor.

The population of the Southern States in 1860 was as follows:

Total white population in all Southern States, 8,179,356.

Total slave population in the Southern States, 3,948,713.

Free population of Virginia in 1860, 1,047,411.

Slave population of Virginia in 1860, 490,865.

From this table it can be seen that the slave population of the South in 1860 was less than half the size of the white population; and the number of slaves relative to the number of whites was about the same for Virginia as for the South taken as a whole. Less than one-third of the population of Virginia in 1860 were slaves.

The total number of slaveholders in the Southern States in 1860 was 383,050; the total number of slaveholders in Virginia at this time was 52,128. If we multiply the number of slaveholders by five, which is considered the average size of a family, we will get the whole number of white people in all the Southern States who were directly served by the slaves, and hence the whole number who profited by slave labor. In all the Southern States, out of a free population of 8,179,356, there could not have been more than 1,918,-185 who had slaves to work for them at all. In Virginia, out of a total white population of 1,047,411, there were only 260,000, or about one-fourth of the white population, who received any of the benefits of slave labor. Then, according to Mr. McMaster, there were 6,266,171, or more than three-fourths of the white people of the South, who received none of the benefits of slave labor, and yet scorned honest toil and held in contempt any white man who tried to make an honest living by hand work.

From the census reports of 1860 it is quite certain that not more than 300,000 of the 900,000 farmers of the South owned any slaves at all; and a large number of those who owned slaves owned only one slave. How did these 600,000 farmers farm without doing manual labor?

The census of 1860 gives the number of people engaged in the different occupations throughout the United States. In Ohio, Virginia, Vermont, and Mississippi we find the following numbers of the free populations engaged in manual labor:

| STATE. | Ohio. | Virginia. | Vermont. | Mississippi. |
|---|---|---|---|---|
| Free population...................... | 2,339,511 | 1,105,453 | 314,369 | 346,674 |
| Total number of free population engaged in manual labor............ | 337,259 | 249,649 | 40,437 | 27,526 |

These four States are selected for comparison because they are typical. The population of Ohio, as can be seen from the table, was more than double the free population of Virginia. In proportion to free population, Virginia had about the same amount of capital invested in manufacturing as Ohio. In both States, however, agriculture was preëminently the leading industry.

The free populations of Mississippi and Vermont were about the same. Neither State had a city of 8,000 population in 1860. The people in these two States engaged in agriculture almost exclusively. Mississippi, however, was one of the richest States in the Union, and Vermont was one of the poorest. The *per capita* wealth in Mississippi in 1860 (counting only the free population) was $1,686.06, while the *per capita* wealth of Vermont was $386.06. It is important to take this into consideration, since naturally a very much larger proportion of the people engaged in manual labor in a poor community than in a rich community.

By reference to the census reports it can be seen that every kind of business activity was found in the Southern States at this time. The Southern people in 1860 were found at work in all kinds of gainful occupations, just as they are to-day, and there was no difference whatever in the attitudes of the Southern and Northern white people with reference to manual labor in general.

### Ohio and Virginia.

The census reports show that almost every kind of manual labor found in Ohio was followed in Virginia, and that some employments were followed in Virginia which were not found in Ohio.  As a rule there is no great disparity in the numbers engaged in the different occupations in the respective States.  When we compare the number of free people in the two States engaged in gainful occupations (manual labor), we find that one out of every 3.71 of the free population of Virginia was thus employed, and one out of every 3.62 in Ohio.

Not so large a number relatively were employed in manual labor in Virginia as in Ohio.  The reason for the slight difference is very evident.  In Virginia the slaves did manual labor exclusively, almost all the servants were slaves, a very large proportion of the farm hands were slaves, and the slaves did much of the blacksmithing and rough carpenter work.  The effect of this was to make the demand relatively less for manual labor of the lower order in Virginia than in Ohio, and hence the larger proportion of the free population prepared themselves for the higher employment.  This fact is plainly brought out in a comparison of Vermont and Mississippi.

|  | Vermont. | Mississippi. |
|---|---|---|
| Number of free people engaged in manual labor | 40,439 | 27,526 |
| Number of servants | 9,463 | 416 |
| Number of farmers | 38,967 | 46,308 |
| Number of students | 528 | 2,242 |

In Vermont 9,463 of the 40,439 people engaged in manual labor were servants; in Mississippi only 416 of those engaged in manual labor were recorded as servants.  Of course the slaves did this work in Mississippi.  In Mississippi there were 7,341 more farmers than in Vermont; and the farmers were not recorded in the census as those engaged in manual labor.  In Mississippi there were nearly five times as many students recorded in the census as in Vermont.

Taking the Southern States as a whole, we find from the census reports that 1,002,409 of the population (free) were engaged in manual labor in 1860.  Farmers, clerks, grocers, merchants, barkeepers, boarding house keepers, innkeepers, liverymen, overseers, are not mentioned in this estimate, except in one State the clerks are counted.  Many of these were engaged in manual labor.

From the facts already brought out and from others that will be given later, it is very clear that manual labor of all kinds was engaged in and honored by the white people of the South before the Civil

War just as it was in the North. The only exception was that the white people of the South would not do menial work for "hire." The real Southerners have changed but little in this since the war. Their attitude to work is about the same to-day that it was in 1860. The Southern white man will hire to drive a road wagon, but he will not drive a carriage; he will curry a mule, but he will not brush a gentleman's coat; he will sweep the streets, but he will not sweep a man's floor; he will feed horses, but he will not wait on the table; he will plow, grub, split rails, but he will not blacken any man's shoes. The Southern white girl will work in a cotton factory twelve hours a day at starvation wages, but she will not cook or be a servant in the home of another, however high the wages or however light the work. All kinds of menial work Southern white men and white women will do in their own homes and for their own people, and even for others when no pay is received; but they would not before the war, and as a rule they will not to-day, do any kind of work which in its nature tends to bring about social inequality between the employer and the employee.

### 5. RAILROAD-BUILDING.

"When it is considered that the power of steam on iron rails and in the water and the multiplied forces of industry created by invention in aid of mechanical art meant the accelerated growth of the West, . . . in almost none of these things did the South as a section have any direct share whatever. The South stood still while the rest of the country had undergone profound changes." (Woodrow Wilson, D. and R., pp. 127, 212, 245.)

The first railroad track laid in the United States was laid on Southern soil in 1828. The first street car system in the United States was established in a Southern State. The first electric street car line in this country was built in Richmond, Va. The progress in railroad-building in the South before the Civil War is shown by the following table:

RAILROADS IN THE UNITED STATES BEFORE THE CIVIL WAR.

|  | No. Miles in 1850. | No. Miles in 1860. | Increase. |
|---|---|---|---|
| Southern States | 2,335.98 | 10,712.66 | 8,376.68 |
| New England States | 2,506.48 | 3,669.39 | 1,162.91 |
| The remaining States | 3,746.33 | 16,210.90 | 12,464.57 |
| Virginia | 515.15 | 1,171.16 | 1,056.01 |
| Massachusetts | 1 035.74 | 1,272.96 | 237.22 |

4

In 1850 there was but one New England State that had as many miles of railroad as Virginia; and there were but four States in the Union, outside of the South, that had more miles of railroad than Virginia; and Georgia had more railroad mileage than Virginia. The little State of South Carolina, which was among the very first to build railroads, had more miles of railroad in 1850 than either Maine, Vermont, Rhode Island, Delaware, Indiana, Illinois, or Wisconsin. In 1860 Virginia had passed Massachusetts in railroad mileage, and had about one-half as many miles of railroad as all the New England States combined; and the increase from 1850 to 1860 in the number of miles of railroad constructed was greater in the Old Dominion by ninety-two miles than in all the New England States combined.

The increase in railroad-building was much greater in the South from 1850 to 1860 than in the rest of the country, and the South had by far more railroad mileage in proportion to free population than the rest of the country.

PERCENTAGE INCREASE IN RAILROAD CONSTRUCTION FROM 1850 TO 1860.

Southern States.........................................  350
New England States...................................  46.3
The remaining States of the Union.....................  332

## 6. MANUFACTURING.

"Manufactures there were none [in the South], except here and there an isolated cotton factory or flour mill. The South stood still while the rest of the country had undergone profound changes." (Woodrow Wilson, D. and R., p. 127, 212, 245.)

"The belief that slave labor could not be utilized in mills and factories prevented the introduction of manufactures." (McMaster, Vol. V., p. 227, 228.)

"They [the Southerners] grasped the fact that slavery made the growth of manufacturing in the South impossible." (Tausig, "Tariff History," p. 73.)

"It [the South] could have no part in the economic progress of the nation, and remained in 1860, as it had been in 1790, exclusively an agricultural region." (Bullock, "Economics," p. 27.)

Rapid as was the increase in railroad construction in the Southern States from 1850 to 1860, it was no more remarkable than the increase in manufacturing in these States for this period. In 1850

Virginia had $18,109,143 invested in manufacturing, and employed in this industry 25,790 male and 3,320 female hands. In the same year all the Southern States combined had $90,615,214 invested in manufacturing. In 1860 Virginia had increased the amount of capital invested in manufacturing from $18,109,143 to $26,935,560. This was an increase of nearly $1,000,000 per year for ten years. In all the Southern States combined the increase of capital invested in manufacturing from 1850 to 1860 was from $90,615,214 to $159,-496,592.

In 1860 there were but two of the six New England States that had more capital invested in manufacturing than Virginia. In 1860 the Southern States had almost as much capital invested in manufacturing as was invested in similar industries in New England ten years before.

Since the industrial conditions of the South corresponded more nearly with industrial conditions of the Northwestern States than with the Eastern States, we will compare the amount of capital invested in manufacturing in these two sections. In Virginia and Ohio agriculture was the leading industry, and there was no greater reason for building up manufactures in Virginia than in Ohio.

THE AMOUNT OF CAPITAL INVESTED IN MANUFACTURING PER CAPITA FREE POPULATION IN 1860.

| | |
|---|---|
| Maryland | $34.8 |
| Michigan | 30.4 |
| Ohio | 24.4 |
| Virginia | 24.3 |
| Florida | 23.8 |
| South Carolina | 23.0 |
| Kentucky | 21.0 |
| Wisconsin | 20.4 |
| Louisiana | 19.0 |
| Missouri | 18.7 |
| Georgia | 18.3 |
| Tennessee | 17.7 |
| Alabama | 17.0 |
| Illinois | 16.0 |
| North Carolina | 14.6 |
| Indiana | 13.8 |
| Minnesota | 13.8 |
| Mississippi | 13.3 |
| Iowa | 10.7 |
| Texas | 7.7 |
| Arkansas | 4.0 |

PERCENTAGE INCREASE IN AMOUNT OF CAPITAL INVESTED IN MANUFACTURING
FROM 1850 TO 1860.

New England States.................................... 55
The six New England States and N. Y., Pa., and N. J........ 72
Southern States......................................... 76

This great relative increase in manufacturing in the Southern
States from 1850 to 1860 was made in spite of the fact that the
Northern States had greatly the advantage of the South with
reference to procuring labor to carry on these industries. Into the
Northern cities and towns hundreds of thousands of immigrants
came annually, and were ready and anxious to work at almost any
price.

The relative disadvantage under which the Southern manufacturer labored with reference to labor is well shown in the average daily wages paid to carpenters in the several States in 1860.
The carpenter may be taken as fairly representative of mechanics in
general. The average price per day paid carpenters in 1860 was as
follows:

The Southern States...............................................$2 04
New England States................................................ 1 61
The United States, excluding Southern States, Cal., and Ore.......... 1 67

SOME OF THE MANUFACTURES IN VIRGINIA IN 1860.

| FACTORIES. | No. Establish-ments. | No. Hands Em-ployed. | Capital In-vested. |
|---|---|---|---|
| Machinery, steam engines, etc...... | 20 | 864 | $ 417,047 |
| Tobacco ......................... | 261 | 11,382 | 3,856,990 |
| Carriages........................ | 127 | 954 | 320,075 |
| Wagons, carts, etc............... | 186 | 500 | 180,855 |
| Leather ......................... | 305 | 780 | 983,033 |
| Flour and meal................... | 1,383 | 2,241 | 5,986,060 |
| Sawed lumber .................... | 779 | 2,114 | 1,283,286 |
| Woolen goods.................... | 45 | 494 | 462,600 |
| Cotton goods ................... | 16 | 1,441 | 1,367,543 |
| Boots and shoes................. | 258 | 1,032 | 258,622 |
| Men's clothing.................. | 63 | 593 | 158,850 |
| Wool carding.................... | 63 | 78 | 59,970 |
| Saddlery and harness............ | 140 | 363 | 138,374 |
| Paper .......................... | 9 | 149 | 154,500 |
| Printing........................ | 22 | 136 | 94,000 |
| Hats and caps................... | 18 | 36 | 31,700 |
| Iron bloom...................... | 1 | 14 | 27,000 |
| Pig iron ....................... | 16 | 529 | 616,405 |
| Bar, sheet, and railroad iron...... | 20 | 1,382 | 1,047,725 |
| Salt ........................... | 14 | 445 | 523,800 |
| Locomotive engines.............. | 1 | 30 | 20,000 |
| Hemp and Manila cordage......... | 2 | 13 | 4,500 |
| Coal mines...................... | 22 | 1,190 | 2,191,400 |
| Hemp bagging................... | ............ | ............ | ............ |
| Turpentine..................... | ............ | ............ | ............ |
| Etc............................ | ............ | ............ | ............ |
| Etc............................ | ............ | ............ | ............ |
| Etc............................ | ............ | ............ | ............ |

### 7. PROGRESS IN AGRICULTURE.

"The system of slave labor condemned the South not only to remain agricultural, but also to prosecute agriculture at the cost of a tremendous waste of resources." (Woodrow Wilson, D. and R., p. 147.)

The remarkable activity shown in the construction of railroads and in building up the manufacturing interests in the South just before the Civil War did not mean any less activity in the development of agriculture. The best way to determine the progress or retrogression of an agricultural community is to note the increase or decrease in the cash valuation of farming land in such communities. From the census of 1860 we see that the percentage increase in the cash valuation of farms from 1850 to 1860 was as follows:

The Southern States..................................... 129
New England States...................................... 27
The remaining States of the Union...................... 102

The amount of increase in the cash valuation of farms from 1850 to 1860 for the following States was as follows:

Virginia .............................................$155,360,118
The six New England States..................... 103,845,294

The increase in the valuation of farms from 1850 to 1860 in either Mississippi, Louisiana, Alabama, Tennessee, Kentucky, or Missouri was much greater than in all the New England States combined.

The free population of the Southern States was several millions less than one-half of the population of the Northern and Western States. Yet the Southern States had in 1860 44,038,478 head of live stock, valued at $512,008,364; while all the other States of the Union combined had only 44,495,924 head of live stock, valued at $568,750,012. The total number of live stock in Virginia was 4,016,-285, while the total number of live stock in the six New England States combined was only 3,938,065. The number of head and the valuation of the live stock in the different sections give a very good basis for comparing the general condition of the farmers in these sections.

### 8. BANKING INSTITUTIONS IN THE SOUTH IN 1860.

"The wealth of the Southern States was not in money wealth: the planters had no money till their crops were sold, and most of what they received then had to be devoted to the payment of what they had borrowed in anticipation of the harvest." (Woodrow Wilson, D. and R., p. 245.)

In a section of country chiefly agricultural we do not expect to find the banking business so extensive as in manufacturing and commercial centers. In a great many farming sections banks are used very little, whereas in towns and cities they are used by almost every one. Notwithstanding this, we find that the banking business in the Southern States in 1860 compared most favorably with that in the rest of the country. In comparing the banking business of the South with the banking business of the North, New York should not be considered, and is not considered in this comparison, since New York was the financial center of the whole country, and as such belonged to no one section. Then, if we compare the banking business of the South with the banking business of the North and West, with New York omitted, we get the following:

|  | Southern States. | Northern and Western States. |
|---|---|---|
| Amount of capital invested in bank *per capita* (free population). | $15.4 | $10.8 |
| Amount of loans *per capita* | 25.00 | 18.7 |
| Amount of deposits *per capita* | 7.9 | 5.5 |
| Increase in Banking Business from 1850 to 1860. |  |  |
| Capital invested in banks | 61% | 63% |
| Loans | 61% | 58% |
| Deposits | 100% | 90% |

Progress in banking is not best shown by increase in capital stock, but by increase in the amount of loans and deposits.

In 1860 Virginia had sixty-five banks, with a total capital stock of $16,005,156; loans, $24,975,782; deposits, $47,729,652. The banking business of Virginia at this time was more than equal to that of Ohio, Illinois, Iowa, Michigan, and Delaware combined.

## 9. BUILDING CITIES.

"The system of slave labor condemned the South to remain agricultural." (Woodrow Wilson, D. and R., p. 127.)

"The South remained in 1860, as it had been in 1790, exclusively an agricultural region." (Bullock, "Economics," p. 27.)

With such activity as has been described, we would naturally expect to find the traces of some towns and cities in the South in 1860. In comparing the relative activities of the North and South at this period in city-building, several things must be taken into consideration, or the South will suffer unjustly in the comparison. One important reason for the very rapid growth of Northern cities and the relatively slow growth of Southern cities was the fact that practically all the immigrants settled in the Northern States. Since the immigrants landed in the cities, the cities were constantly supplied with all the labor that was demanded, and this made their rapid growth easy. The foreigner was a tremendous factor in building Northern cities. A very large part of the progress of the North before the Civil War was due not to any superiority of the native Northern people over the Southerners, but was due to the fact that the millions of immigrants settled in that section. New York State alone in 1860 had twice as many foreigners as all of the fourteen Southern States combined. Massachusetts had one-half as many as all the Southern States combined, and Ohio, Illinois, and Wisconsin each had more than half as many foreigners as lived in all the Southern States.

The people to whom the South looked almost exclusively to increase the population of the towns and cities were the native American farmers living in the Southern States. These people in many cases were living on farms which had been tilled by their fathers and grandfathers, and they were fairly well contented with their lot. They had never known anything but the country, and they were very reluctant to leave the old associations for a life that was unknown to them. Notwithstanding the many disadvantages that confronted the South in building cities, the progress in this direction was rapid after 1830, and was in keeping with the general interests of a progressive community. In 1860 there were thirty cities in the Southern States of 8,000 population and over. The number in each State was as follows:

| | |
|---|---|
| Alabama | 2 |
| Georgia | 5 |
| Kentucky | 4 |
| Louisiana | 3 |
| Maryland | 2 |
| Missouri | 3 |
| North Carolina | 1 |
| South Carolina | 1 |

| | |
|---|---|
| Tennessee .................................................... | 2 |
| Texas ....................................................... | 1 |
| Virginia ..................................................... | 6 |
| Total ................................................. | 30 |

The average population of these thirty cities was 33,331. Many towns in the South of less than 8,000 population had all the characteristics of the city. This was far more true of the South than of the North, because a larger number of farmers and others of this class lived in the towns in the North, whereas all such people lived in the country in the South.

The total city population of the Southern States in 1860 was 999,947. Nearly one-eighth of the entire white population of the South lived in cities in 1860. Three out of the eight largest cities in the United States in 1860 were in Southern States; four out of the eleven largest cities were in the South. Of the six States having the largest city population, two of these were Southern; and of the eleven States having the largest city population, five were Southern. If we arrange the States of the Union according to the percentage of their whole free population living in cities of 8,000 people and over, placing that State first having the largest per cent of its free population in cities, and so on down, we get the following results:

| | | |
|---|---|---|
| 1. Rhode Island. | 12. Ohio. | 23. Alabama. |
| 2. Louisiana. | 13. Kentucky. | 24. Tennessee. |
| 3. Massachusetts. | 14. South Carolina. | 25. Texas. |
| 4. New York. | 15. Illinois. | 26. North Carolina. |
| 5. Maryland. | 16. Virginia. | 27. Mississippi. |
| 6. New Jersey. | 17. Georgia. | 28. Kansas. |
| 7. Connecticut. | 18. Michigan. | 29. Vermont. |
| 8. Pennsylvania. | 19. Maine. | 30. Florida. |
| 9. Delaware. | 20. Minnesota. | 31. Arkansas. |
| 10. New Hampshire. | 21. Indiana. | 32. Oregon. |
| 11. Missouri. | 22. Iowa. | |

If we compare Virginia with Ohio, we find that the city population of Virginia, in proportion to the free population of the State, was almost equal to that of Ohio. The same was true of Kentucky, Georgia, and South Carolina. Three of the Southern States led Ohio in city population in proportion to their free population. The industrial conditions of the South were similar to those in Ohio, and there was no greater demand for cities in the South than in Ohio. At the opening of the war the South had built cities in every section of the country. In Maryland they had built the fourth largest city in the United States; in Virginia they had built six cities with an aggregate population of 107,071; in the far South they had built New Orleans with a population of 168,675—about the size of Boston—and Charleston with a population of over 40,-ooo, and Memphis with a population of over 22,000, and Mobile with a population of nearly 30,000, and Savannah with a population of over 22,000, and Augusta with a population of over 12,000; in the Southwest they had built Nashville with a population of nearly 17,-ooo, and Louisville with a population of over 68,000. The largest city in the far North was Boston, with a population of 177,840; the largest city in the far South was New Orleans, with a population of 168,675.

The best proof of the activity and capacity of the Southern people in adapting themselves to the new economic conditions brought about by steam and railroads is shown by their experience in city-building in the West. When the great West was opened, people from New England, New York, and Pennsylvania passed into the Northwest and settled; and the people from Virginia, North Carolina, South Carolina, Tennessee, and Kentucky emigrated to the Southwest. Here we had the Northern men side by side with the Southerners in a new country, with opportunities and conditions practically the same for both. The only difference worth considering was that the Southerners had slaves and the Northern people did not have slaves. A great city in the West was needed, and this great city was built on Southern soil. St. Louis in 1860 had a population of 160,773—a great city for those days—and it had been only a few years in building. In the great Northwest, settled by the New Englanders and people from other Northern States, there was not a single city worth mentioning when the war opened. Even Chicago at that time had but 109,260 population.

The increase in population from 1850 to 1860 for the following Southern cities, Baltimore, Richmond, Savannah, Mobile, New Orleans, Memphis, Nashville, Covington, Louisville, St. Louis, Charleston, was forty-seven per cent. The increase in population for the same period for the five largest Northern cities—namely, New York, Brooklyn, Philadelphia, Boston, and Cincinnati—was fifty per cent. If we compare the growth of Boston, the distinctively Northern city, with the growth of New Orleans, the distinctively Southern city, from 1850 to 1860, we find that New Orleans increased in population forty-five per cent, while the increase in the population of Boston for the same period was but twenty-nine per cent. The leading Southern cities were growing about as rapidly as the leading Northern cities, notwithstanding the relative disadvantages under which they labored. New York should not be considered in this comparison, because it was as much a product of the South as of the West. New York really belongs to the whole country.

### 10. PER CAPITA WEALTH.

"The system [slave labor] produced one of the most singular non-productive classes that any country has ever seen. This was a class known in the South as the poor whites. Free, but on that account shut out from laboring for others both because of their pride of freedom and because of the absence of any system of hired labor." (Woodrow Wilson, D. and R., p. 128.)

"The mean whites comprised about seven-tenths of the whole white population of the South. They are in a condition little removed from savage life." [Professor Cairns, "Slave Power" (written before 1860), Harper's, Vol. XXIX., p. 123.]

"They [poor whites] were the most lazy, the most idle, the most shiftless, the most worthless of men. Work of every kind they abhorred." (McMaster, Vol. II., p. 14.)

Perhaps the best way to estimate the relative producing power and thrift and frugality of two or more communities is by a comparison of the *per capita* wealth. To be perfectly fair in making such a comparison, proper allowances must be made for all peculiar conditions in the respective communities which might militate for or against such communities in comparing them one with another.

The population of the Southern States in 1860 was as follows:

| | |
|---|---|
| Free population | 8,179,356 |
| Slave population | 3,948,713 |
| Total population | 12,128,069 |

Then about one-third of the population of the South in 1860 were African slaves. It is conceded by all that the negro in any state is very much inferior as a worker to the American white man. It is also conceded that free labor is far more productive than slave labor even when there is no difference in capacity between the slaves and the freemen. Then some allowance should be made in favor of the South in this comparison on account of the natural inferiority of one-third of the population.

In Virginia and in the other Southern States where agriculture was the principal industry almost no labor-saving machines were used in production before the Civil War. There were two reasons for this. In the first place, very little machinery was used in agriculture anywhere in this country before the Civil War; and, in the second place, machinery could not have been used to an advantage by the careless, stupid slaves of the South.

The essential characteristic of a machine is its labor-saving quality; it does the work formerly done by "hands," it saves labor, it takes the place of men. In manufacturing, different from agriculture, machinery was used extensively long before 1860. Hence in the manufacturing sections, as in New England, New York, Pennsylvania, New Jersey, etc., machines took the place of men and did the work formerly done by "hands." In Virginia and in the other Southern States, as well as in the Western States, men—"hands"—were used in the place of machinery.

But making no allowance for the inferiority of the slave, and no allowance for the advantage of the labor-saving machines in certain sections of the North in the accumulation of wealth, we get the following:

Per capita wealth in Southern States in 1860 (not counting slaves in population)..............................$812 80

Per capita wealth in Southern States (counting slaves in population).................................... 557 00

Per capita wealth in Northern and Western States...... 489 00

Of the three richest States in the Union in 1860, two of them were Southern States (Louisiana and South Carolina). Of the five richest States in the Union, three were Southern; of the ten richest States in the Union, six were Southern; of the seventeen richest States in the Union, ten were Southern States. The Southern white people in 1860 possessed almost twice as much property in proportion to population as was possessed by the Northern and Western people.

### REFERENCES.

Eighth Census United States, Vol. Agriculture, pp. 10, 180-190, 221, 247.

Eighth Census United States, Vol. Population, pp. 399, 524, 525, 599, 593, 595, 519, 607.

Eighth Census United States, Vol. Manufactures, pp. 760, 759.

Eighth Census United States, Compendium, pp. 192, 193, 197, 214-235.
Eighth Census United States, Vol. Mortality, etc., pp. 295, 512.
Railroad Transportation, Hadley, p. 32.
Miss Roland's Life of George Mason, Vol. I., pp. 101 and 102.
Meades's Old Churches, Vol. I., p. 98.

The fact that a large portion of the wealth of the South was in slaves should not be taken into consideration at all in making this comparison. ( The slaves were not given to the Southern people, neither were they taken by force by them. They were brought to the South by Northern men, and sold at their market value just as horses and cows and manufactured products were sold to the Southerners from nonslaveholding States. In return for all these slaves the New Englander received money and products from the South of an equivalent value, and carried these back to invest in buildings and machines and ships. ) The Southerner, as the New Englander, could have invested his money in other than slave property if he had so desired ; and he might have accumulated more had he done this. As has been seen, slavery gave him no special advantage over those who invested in a different kind of property. If the slaves had been emancipated peaceably, of course the slaveholders would have received from the government the full value of their slaves, and hence their *per capita* wealth would have been the same after emancipation as before. If property rights in lands were abolished in the Northern States to-day without any compensation to the owner, the "public wealth" would not be reduced thereby directly, but millions of men would be driven into bankruptcy, and the Northern people would receive a blow that would injure them for years to come, and would make them poor indeed as compared with communities which had never held property rights in lands.

One of the most convincing proofs that it was not in the institution of slavery but in the capacity of the white people of the South that this great wealth was accumulated is found in the relative progress of the Southern States in the accumulation of wealth since the war. In this comparison Missouri and Maryland are not taken into consideration. In 1860 the true valuation of real and personal property was about the same in the Southern States as it was in the six New England States and New York, Pennsylvania, and New Jersey. In 1870 the South had less than one-fifth the wealth of these nine Northern States. But ten years later the South had more than a third as much wealth as these Northern

States; and in 1890 the relative increase of wealth had been so great that the true valuation of real and personal property in these Southern States was almost half that of the nine Northern States here considered. If this relative increase continues, it will not be long before the South will regain the relative place she held before the Civil War with reference to the amount of wealth possessed.

II. A MORE INTENSIVE INVESTIGATION BASED ON VIRGINIA RECORDS.

The conclusions thus far reached in this investigation with reference to industrial conditions have been based very largely on the census reports. While the census reports furnish us the most complete and the most reliable data that can be had, these will not be depended on exclusively in this work. The land and property books in Virginia, together with other similar documents which have been preserved, contain the facts from which the true economic history of this section can be written. A very thorough investigation has been made of these documents in certain representative counties in Virginia, and an epitome of the results of this investigation is here given. If the conclusions thus reached corroborate the conclusions based on the facts brought out in the census reports, our position will be greatly strengthened.

For this investigation two groups of counties in Virginia have been chosen. The counties selected represent every section of the State. In the first group of counties the investigation has been more intensive and more extensive than in the second. The most thorough investigation has been made in Henry County.

In each group the counties are arranged in the order of proportionate slave population. The county having the largest number of slaves in proportion to white population is placed first, and the other counties follow in order. The two counties in the first group —Amelia and Henry—that have the largest proportion of slave population had also the largest number of big slaveholders. The number of slaves given as belonging to each slaveholder does not represent the whole number of slaves owned by each, since slaves under twelve years of age do not appear in the property books, and hence are not counted in this investigation.

These counties represent every section of the State, and represent every phase of slavery found in Virginia. In Amelia County the slave population was three times as large as the white population, and more than seventy per cent of the white males over twenty-one years of age in this county owned slaves.  In Washington County the white population was nearly six times as large as the slave population, and only fourteen per cent of the white males twenty-one years of age and older were slaveholders.  Between these two extremes the other counties investigated give widely varying proportions of white and slave populations.  Only two counties in the State had a larger slave population than Pittsylvania, and Albemarle County had almost as many slaves as Pittsylvania.  Henry County had more big slaveholders—i. e., slaveholders owning more than one hundred slaves each—in proportion to population than any other county in the State with only one exception, yet the large majority of the white people of Henry owned no slaves.  Surely whatever was good and whatever was bad in slavery anywhere in the South were found somewhere in the life of the people in these counties.  If the conclusions of the historians as to the horrible effects of slavery on the life of the white people in the South are sound, these counties ought to corroborate them.

It is plain that small landowners were in the majority everywhere. In the first group of counties the majority of landowners owned less than two hundred acres of land; and this was perhaps true in the second group of counties.  In Henry County, preëminently the county of the big slaveholders, the majority of the landowners owned from fifty to two hundred acres.  In this county there were three hundred and fifteen people owning land who owned no slaves.  These figures indicate that there were many farmers in big slaveholding counties, owning farms of considerable size, who owned no slaves; and they further indicate that nothing like land monopoly was in existence in any of these counties.  In the table that follows it is seen that the number of landowners was on the increase in every county investigated with but one exception, notwithstanding the large emigration to the west at this time.

| Group I. | White Population. | Slave Population. | No. White Males over 21 Years Old. | No. Slave Owners. | No. Owning One Slave. | No. Owning Five Slaves. | Per Cent of White Males over 21 Years Old Owning Slaves. | Per Cent of White Males Over 21 Years Old Owning Land. | Average Value of Land per Acre. |
|---|---|---|---|---|---|---|---|---|---|
| Amelia........ | 2,897 | 7,655 | 677 | 486 | 113 | 255 | 71.7 | 85.3 | $ 9 81 |
| Henry......... | 6,773 | 5,018 | 1,454 | 480 | 154 | 354 | 33. | 54.6 | ...... |
| Pittsylvania ... | 17,105 | 14,340 | 3,253 | 1,225 | ...... | ...... | 37.6 | ...... | ...... |
| Bedford ....... | 14,388 | 10,176 | 3,013 | 1,098 | 327 | 798 | 36.4 | 61.3 | 12 00 |
| Campbell...... | 13,588 | 8,886 | 1,921 | 866 | 230 | 601 | 45. | 69.4 | ...... |
| Franklin...... | 13,692 | 6,351 | 2,628 | 668 | 251 | 484 | 25.4 | 67.5 | ...... |
| Roanoke...... | 5,250 | 2,643 | 1,156 | 311 | 107 | 234 | 18 2 | 69.2 | 15 30 |
| Washington ... | 6,500 | 1,100 | 1,257 | 177 | 57 | 145 | 14. | ...... | 10 00 |
| **Group II.** | | | | | | | | | |
| Culpepper..... | 4,959 | 6,675 | 991 | ...... | ...... | ...... | ...... | 90.2 | 13 03 |
| Hanover. .... | 7,482 | 9,483 | 1,256 | ...... | ...... | ...... | ...... | 100. | 10 90 |
| Albemarle..... | 12,103 | 13,916 | 2,420 | ...... | ...... | ...... | ...... | 65.7 | 15 19 |
| Chesterfield . .. | 10,019 | 8,354 | 2,003 | ...... | ...... | ...... | ...... | 80.8 | ...... |
| Isle of Wight .. | 5,037 | 3,570 | 1,006 | ...... | ...... | ...... | ...... | 100. | 6 86 |
| Montgomery .. | 8,251 | 2,219 | 1,650 | ...... | ...... | ...... | ...... | 48.7 | ...... |

THE AMOUNT OF CAPITAL INVESTED IN MINING OR MANUFACTURING IN 1860 ACCORDING TO THE PROPERTY BOOKS IN SOME OF THE COUNTIES.

Henry County............................................$85,000
Pittsylvania County.................................... 35,700
Franklin County........................................ 50,634
Roanoke County........................................ 41,265

The above amounts do not represent all of the manufacturing done in the counties named. In this investigation no account is taken of manufacturing done in towns.

TOTAL VALUE OF MONEY, BONDS, CLAIMS, ETC., IN SOME OF THE COUNTIES.

Amelia County......................................$ 528,591
Henry County........................................ 286,915
Pittsylvania County................................. 1,155,950
Franklin County...................................... 443,996
Roanoke County...................................... 427,565

The lowest average price of land, with but one exception, was in Amelia County, where the proportion of slaves and the proportion of slave owners were greatest; while the highest average price of land, with but one exception, was in Roanoke County, where the number of slaves and the number of slave owners were relatively small. The lowest average price of land was in Isle of Wight County, one of the eight original shires in extreme Tide Water Virginia. We can hardly conclude from this that the nonslaveholders were driven away from all good lands, as the historians tell us they were.

The conclusions here reached with reference to the economic conditions in Virginia in 1860 are in complete accord with the conclusions based on the facts brought out in the census reports. There is not a single fact in all of this investigation that can be used in any way to support the theory of the historians that there was a landed-slave aristocracy. On the other hand, every fact is in direct opposition to such a theory. The proof is almost absolutely positive that the greatest democracy prevailed in industry, and that the way was open for every man to rise as high as his merit deserved. All the facts show that the people of these sections were energetic, frugal, and efficient.

CONCLUSION.

1. In the South in 1860 there was a larger number of farms containing between three and five hundred acres, in proportion to the free population, than in the North.

2. The white population of the South were engaged in all kinds of manual labor before the war with the exception of menial service.

3. The South had a larger number of miles of railroad in 1860, in proportion to her free population, than the rest of the country; and the increase in railroad construction was greater in the South from 1850 to 1860 than in the rest of the country.

4. In 1860 the Southern people were engaged in almost all kinds of manufacturing. In 1860 the Southern States had almost as much capital invested in manufacturing as all the New England States had invested in this industry ten years before, and the percentage increase in manufacturing was greater in the South from 1850 to 1860 than in the rest of the country.

5. In 1860 the cash value of farms was considerably larger in the South, in proportion to the free population, than in the rest of the country; and the increase in the value of farms from 1850 to 1860 was much greater in the South than in the North and West.

6. The South was far in advance of the rest of the country both in the number and in the value of live stock.

7. The South had a larger amount of capital invested in banks in 1860 than the Northern States, and was doing a larger banking

business, and the increase in banking business from 1850 to 1860 was greater in the South than in the rest of the country.

8. The South was by far the richest section of this country in 1860.

9. Wages were higher in the South than in the North in 1860.

10. The South had thirty cities in 1860 with a total population of nearly 1,000,000, and three of them were among the eight largest cities in the United States.

### REFERENCES.

Land and Property Books, etc., in Henry County, Va., Clerk's Office.
Land and Property Books, etc., in Franklin County, Va., Clerk's Office.
Land and Property Books, etc., in Pittsylvania County, Va., Clerk's Office.
Land and Property Books, etc., in Campbell County, Va., Clerk's Office.
Land and Property Books, etc., in Bedford County, Va., Clerk's Office.
Land and Property Books, etc., in Roanoke County, Va., Clerk's Office.
Land and Property Books, etc., in Washington County, Va., Clerk's Office.
Land and Property Books, etc., in Amelia County, Va., Clerk's Office.
Land Books in Virginia State Library of Culpeper County.
Land Books in Virginia State Library of Hanover County.
Land Books in Virginia State Library of Albemarle County.
Land Books in Virginia State Library of Chesterfield County.
Land Books in Virginia State Library of Isle of Wight County.
Land Books in Virginia State Library of Montgomery County.

5

# IV. THE EDUCATIONAL MOVEMENT IN THE SOUTH BEFORE THE CIVIL WAR.

---

## I. EDUCATION IN GENERAL.

"Without Church, university, schools, or literature in any form that required or fostered intellectual life, the Virginians concentrated their thoughts almost exclusively upon politics." (Henry Adams, "History of the United States," Vol. II., p. 138.)

"The lack of schools [in the South] was painfully apparent." (Rhodes, "History of the United States," Vol. II., pp. 349, 350.)

"Every one knew that the schools in the South were rare and poor." (Andrews, "History of the United States," Vol. II., pp. 4, 5.)

We have seen that the South was certainly not behind the rest of the country in the development of her material resources in 1860. The material developments of the Southern States from 1850 to 1860 has perhaps never been surpassed by any other section of this country in any similar period. But what was the South doing for education at this time?

In 1860 the Southern States, in proportion to population, had more than twice as many students in college as New England, and the colleges of the South had nearly twice the income of those in New England. Not only did the South lead New England and the rest of the country in the amount spent annually for college education, but the Southern States were also far in advance of these sections in the total amount spent annually for public schools, academies, and other schools not including colleges. The average amount spent in the South annually for all educational purposes was about one-tenth more, in proportion to free population, than was spent in New England for educational purposes, and nearly one-third more than the rest of the country spent for all educational purposes.

| 1860. | Southern States. | New England States. | Remaining States. |
|---|---|---|---|
| Number colleges for each 100,000 population.... | 27.3 | 6.7 | 11.5 |
| Number college teachers for each 100,000 free population .............................. | 158.8 | 74.9 | 73.4 |
| Number college students for each 1,000 free population...................................... | 28.8 | 11.9 | 15.7 |
| Amount annual income of colleges for each 100 free population............................. | $ 18 00 | $ 11 10 | $ 7 10 |
| Amount income from endowment of all schools, save public schools, for each 100 free population. ........................................ | 97 10 | 95 07 | 43 10 |
| Average amount spent annually for each 100 free population for public schools............ | 66 50 | 83 50 | 74 90 |
| Average amount spent annually for each 100 free population for public schools, academies, and other schools, not including colleges. .... | 125 10 | 118 80 | 101 10 |
| Average amount annually spent for all educational purposes for each 100 free population... | 143 10 | 129 90 | 108 20 |

—Eighth U. S. Census Mortality, etc., pp. 502-509.

## 2. THE PUBLIC SCHOOLS.

"In the United States the public school system has been extended throughout the Southern States, where, previous to the Civil War, there was no free school system for the whites." (Lyman Abbott, "Christianity and Social Problems," p. 38.)

### PUBLIC SCHOOLS IN THE UNITED STATES IN 1860.

| | No. Schools. | No. Teachers. | No. Pupils. | Annual Income. |
|---|---|---|---|---|
| Southern States ......... | 27,582 | 29,179 | 954,678 | $ 5,269,642 |
| New England States..... | 15,738 | 16,978 | 653,234 | 2,972,828 |
| Other States............. | 64,209 | 81,527 | 3,335,926 | 14,240,842 |

A failure to draw a clear distinction between public schools and State public schools, and public free schools and private free schools, and free education for certain classes in private schools and public schools, has been the cause of much confusion and of great misunderstanding on the whole question of popular education in the United States. This distinction has not been clearly made by any one, as far as the writer knows. The public schools may or may not be free; they may be directed by the State, or by the locality in which they are situated. The State may provide free education in public schools or free education in private schools.

When it is stated that the New England colonies had a public school system and that the Southern colonies did not have a public school system, it cannot be inferred from this that the New England colonies had a larger number of schools or more efficient schools or cheaper schools or more popular schools, or that the New England colonies were more interested in popular education, than the Southern colonies.

Some of the New England colonies passed laws requiring the towns to provide schools. No appropriations were made by the State, and there was nothing like any central supervision. The schools were not free, and they were public only in the sense that they were directed by the representatives of the respective towns, under mandatory statutes of the colony. The Southern colonies, true to the instinct of local self-government, left the organization of common schools to private initiative in each community. As much can be said for the one system as for the other. The New England public school at this time was in thorough accord with the ecclesiastical policy of this section. It was natural for them to turn away from the liberty of the private school, which had been in vogue so long in England, and put the training of the youth under the watchful oversight of the thoroughly orthodox. The private school of the Southern colonies was in keeping with the idea of liberty characteristic of the Southern people at this time.

As soon as the Southern colonies became States they began at once to provide for State systems of public education. This provision was incorporated in the constitutions of some of the Southern States. Money was appropriated for public education in North Carolina forty years before Massachusetts began to accumulate an educational fund. South Carolina adopted a State public free school system in 1811, and the free schools of Charleston date from the passage of this act; whereas Massachusetts did not begin to organize a State system of public schools till 1837, and some of the New England States, with New York and New Jersey, had not adopted the State free school system in 1860. The State system of free public schools originated in the South, and was in operation more than a half century before it was adopted by a number of Northern States. Other Southern States were as much interested in popular education as South Carolina, but their methods of meeting the problem were different, at least for a while. North Carolina and Louisiana adopted the State public free school system many years before the Civil War. The policy of Virginia and some other Southern States was the same in principle, but the method of adoption deferred the action of the State as a whole for some years. All the Southern States, however, began at a very early date to make provisions for the free education of all the poor children within their borders.

Perhaps no other State in the Union made greater progress in perfecting the State public free school system before the Civil War than North Carolina. Certainly in no other State was the interest in public education deeper or wider than here, and in no other was there greater unanimity on the part of the entire citizenship. In selecting the very small number of men who did most in perfecting the public school system in America, no other man should be given a higher place than Dr. Calvin Henderson Wiley, State Superintendent of Schools for the State of North Carolina from 1852 down to the period of the Civil War. On this roll of honor Horace Mann deserves a high place, but he deserves no higher place than Dr. Wiley.

The Southern States met with various degrees of success and failure in working out the problems of public education before 1860, but their failures were no greater, perhaps, than those in New England. It is probable that there was not a more inefficient system of schools anywhere in this country than was found in the State of Vermont between 1850 and 1860. The writer will here give a brief sketch of the public school movements in some of the States.

### New England Schools.

#### *Massachusetts.*

The general school fund of Massachusetts was established in 1834. In 1837 Massachusetts established the first State Board of Education, and Horace Mann was elected the first secretary. In 1855 only sixty-four per cent of the children between five and fifteen years of age were in the public schools. In 1851 there were 334 schools with more than 70 pupils, and 188 schools with more than 120 pupils under one teacher.

#### *Connecticut.*

The State system of public schools seems to have begun in Connecticut in 1838. But the public schools here were not free. In

1855 the State Superintendent had the following to say: "A majority
of the districts have made little or no progress for many years; the
majority of the schoolhouses are utterly unfit for school purposes;
a majority of the teachers are incompetent." The superintendent
at this time (1855) regarded the rate bill (tuition) the hardship
which was especially felt by the poorer classes.

### Rhode Island.

The State system of schools was established in Rhode Island
in 1843. In the report of the superintendent of 1850 it is stated
that the rate bill (tuition) was one great obstacle in the way of
a more general attendance on schools.

### Vermont.

A State school fund was established in Vermont in 1825, but later
it was abolished, and the amount of money on hand ($250,000) was
applied to the building of a Statehouse. There was a revival of
interest in public schools some years later. In the report of the
Superintendent for the year 1846 the system is terribly arraigned.
The wages of teachers were $12 per month for men, and $4.75 per
month for women, including board. In 1850 seventy per cent of
the teachers were women, and these received $5.62 per month with
board. In 1851 Vermont abolished the office of State Superintendent of Schools, and it was not established again till 1856.

### New Hampshire.

The State system of education was inaugurated in New Hampshire
in 1846. The new movement was regarded by its friends as an
experiment. The average wages of male teachers in 1848, exclusive
of board, was $13.50, and of female teachers, $5.65.

### Maine.

In 1846 the State system of schools was adopted in the State of
Maine. In 1847 the teachers were receiving $15 per month for men,
and $1.20 per week for women. Of the 240,000 children and youths
between the ages of four and twenty-one years, 122,000 in winter
and 95,000 in summer "did not darken schoolhouse doors."

Summing up the conditions in New England just previous to the
Civil War, Dr. Mayo says in the "Report of the Commissioner of

Education for 1897-98:" "New England, then the most progressive portion of the republic, was still educationally lingering in the good old British aristocratic habit of largely depending on a superior educational class to do the thinking and save the people according to some vicarious scheme of public salvation.

### New York.

In 1849-50 the rural districts of the State of New York, by a majority of 47,000 votes in forty-two of the fifty-nine counties, voted against free schools. The city of New York overcame this majority of the country districts, but free schools were not adopted for the State till 1867.

### New Jersey.

In 1850 the people of New Jersey looked to the Legislature to consider the subject of free schools by a general law. It was recommended that a permissive statute be passed authorizing all townships by a vote of two-thirds to establish free schools supported by a local tax. Such a law had been passed in Virginia many years before this time. But there is no indication that New Jersey ever succeeded in getting this law passed before the Civil War.

### PUBLIC SCHOOLS IN THE SOUTH.

### South Carolina.

In 1790 Charleston established the Orphans' Home, with an elementary school attached, which has been supported from its beginning by the city, at an annual expense of $20,000. More than 4,000 orphan children have been educated and protected in its walls. In 1785 the State chartered two colleges and, it appears, made an appropriation for them. In 1801 the Legislature granted $50,000 and an annual subsidy of $6,000 to establish the South Carolina College. In 1811 the Legislature, on petition of several counties, established what was meant to be a working system of free common schools open to all white children of school age. The law provided that, while every white child of suitable age in the district had the right to this instruction, the preference should be given to destitute orphans and the children of the poor in case of a deficiency of funds. Three hundred dollars was appropriated for each school, while the people were required to furnish schoolhouses. One hundred and thirty-three schools were at once established. Up to 1821, $302,-490 had been expended by the State on these State public free schools. The free schools of Charleston date from the passage of this act, in 1811. This was the first free school system founded in America, and it continued with various degrees of success down to the Civil War.

## Louisiana.

In 1811 the Legislature of Louisiana voted $15,000 for the college of Orleans, and $2,000 for one or more schools in each county. New Orleans adopted the public school system in 1841. In 1845 a State free school system was established by the Constitution of the State with the following provisions: "The Legislature shall establish free schools throughout the State, and shall provide means for their support by taxation on property and otherwise." The salary of the State Superintendent of Schools was fixed at $3,000 per annum, with $800 for incidentals. When Horace Mann was elected as the head of the Massachusetts State system of schools, a few years before his salary was fixed at $1,000, with no money allowed for incidental expenses. It is estimated that the State of Louisiana had in 1841 expended $2,000,000 to educate the people. Louisiana also made provision for the establishment of a university in 1845.

## Maryland.

A free school was established by the State of Maryland in a majority of the counties before 1790. A State system of public schools was adopted in 1825.

## Georgia.

The constitution of Georgia of 1777 provided that schools should be erected in each county of the State and supported at the general expense of the State.

## North Carolina.

The constitution of North Carolina of 1776 provided for primary education. The University of North Carolina was chartered in 1789; it was opened in 1795. Gov. James Turner, in his message to the Legislature, November 21, 1804, said: "Knowledge is one of the firmest pillars of national strength. . . . I am desirous of seeing a plan of education introduced which shall extend itself into every corner of the State." Governor Alexander in 1806 indorsed the recommendation of Governor Turner, and added a ringing demand of his own. Governor Hawkins, in his message to the Assembly in 1811, said: "Too much attention cannot be paid to the all-important subject of education. In despotic governments, where the supreme power is in the possession of a tyrant or divided amongst a hereditary aristocracy (generally corrupt and wicked), the ignorance of the people is a security of the people to their rulers; but in free government, where the offices and the honors of the State are open to all, the superiority of these political privileges should be infused into every citizen from his earliest infancy, so as to produce an enthusiastic attachment to his own country and insure a jealous support to their own constitution, laws, and government, to the total exclusion of all foreign influence or partiality. A certain degree of education should be placed within the reach of every child in the State." In 1815 Governor Miller called the attention of the Assembly to the need of public schools.

In 1825 the literary fund of the State was established. From this time on the common schools in North Carolina began to come to the front.

In 1828 the amount of the literary fund was.........$    77,811 62
In 1834 the amount of the literary fund was........   139,403 99
In 1836 the amount of the literary fund was........   242,045 09
In 1838 the amount of the literary fund was........ 1,732,485 00

In 1839 the State system of public schools was put into operation by the Legislature. In 1852 the Legislature passed an act to provide for the appointment of a State Superintendent of Common Schools. The State Superintendent was to be elected by the Legislature, and to hold office for two years. Dr. Wiley, then a member of the Legislature as a Whig, was selected as State Superintendent by the Legislature, which was overwhelmingly Democratic. His salary was fixed at $1,500 per annum.

In 1857 the average length of the school was four months, the average attendance was forty pupils, and the average salary for teachers was about $24 per month. Some teachers received as high as $40 per month. The sum expended in the whole State was about $253,000. The number of certificates to teachers granted and reported was 2,256. About 214 of the number of teachers here given were women. The number of children in attendance was 97,644.

In 1855 the following report was made:

| | |
|---|---|
| Number of students in colleges, about............................. | 1,000 |
| Number of students in academies................................ | 9,000 |
| Number of male colleges......................................... | 5 |
| Number of female colleges....................................... | 9 |
| Number of academies, about..................................... | 300 |
| Number of common schools, about............................... | 3,500 |
| Number of counties in State...................................... | 85 |
| Number of children attending schools in seventy-two counties........ | 112,632 |
| Number of children attending schools in the State, about........... | 130,000 |

In 1856 there were 2,000 teachers who held certificates of character and qualifications from examining committees; all were under the spur of annual examinations.

In 1860 the receipts of school money amounted to $408,556.32. In this year the amount of school taxes collected in the State was about $100,000.

There were during the period of reorganization and growth which began in 1852 two auxiliary agencies in the work of the schools which were of great importance. These agencies, which began before 1860 to take an official character, were the North Carolina Journal of Education and the Educational Association of North Carolina.

In the message of Governor Ellis to the General Assembly of 1860-61 we find the following:

| | |
|---|---|
| Number of colleges (male)........................... | 6 |
| Number of colleges (female)......................... | 13 |
| Number of academies and select schools.............. | 350 |
| Number of primary schools........................... | 4,000 |
| Number of students in colleges (male)................ | 900 |
| Number of students in colleges (female).............. | 1,500 |
| Number of students in academies, etc................. | 15,000 |
| Number of students in primary schools................ | 160,000 |
| Total white population in 1860...................... | 631,100 |

REFERENCES.

Reports of United States Commissioner of Education, 1897-98, Vol. I., pp. 401, 402, 405, 409, 412, 413, 421, 457-472, 458-462, 468; Vol. II., 359-391, 402, 426-432, 394.

Reports of United States Commissioner of Education, 1895-96, Vol. I., pp. 288-293, 274-278, 307-311, 295-299.

Reports of United States Commissioner of Education, 1896-97, Vol. II., 1384-1399, 1400, 1406, 1414, 1425-1453.

Eighth Census United States, Vol. Mortality, etc., pp. 502-509.

## Virginia.

The first free school established on American soil was perhaps in the Colony of Virginia. This school was in operation in 1649, and was liberally endowed. Mr. Jefferson at a very early date had in mind a very elaborate plan of public education for Virginia, but it was not until 1811 that the State made provision for the system of public education. In 1811 the literary fund was created by the Legislature. The object of this fund was the establishment of the University of Virginia and the education of all the free white children in the State.

James Barber was Governor of Virginia in 1812-14. In his death he made the following request of his son: "If anything is put over me, let it be of the plainest granite, with no other claim than this: 'Here lies James Barber, Originator of the Literary Fund of Virginia.'"

The work of public education began in a very short while. The annual income from the fund, as early as 1822, was $45,000.

From the report of the Superintendent of Schools of Henry County, Virginia, in 1838, we learn that 400 children in this county were entitled to the use of the school fund at this time, and that 334 had their tuition paid from this fund. The average price of tuition, exclusive of books, etc., was about four cents for every day's attendance of each poor child. In the report of 1843 the following statement is made: "A majority of the foregoing schools continue in operation ten months in the year. The elementary books principally used are Townes and Webster's spelling book, New York reader, English reader, Grimshaw's History of the United States, Walker's dictionary, Pike's arithmetic, Mitchell and Adams's geography, Murray's grammar, and Parley's geography."

In 1820 the State system of free schools for the poor was inaugurated. A few years later each county and town was permitted by the Legislature to adopt a State free school system. Just when the first county voted to adopt the State free school system for all the children of the county, the writer does not know. But Albemarle and Norfolk Counties, by acts of the Legislature in 1845, were authorized to inaugurate the free school system. We here give a synopsis of an act passed by the Virginia Legislature in 1845: "Whereas the welfare of all nations and the safety of free States are intimately connected with the general diffusion of knowledge amongst the people; and whereas the experience of various countries demonstrates that those systems of public instruction are most efficient wherein the primary schools are supported at the common charge, and freely open to all, and are subject to frequent and rigorous inspection under public authority; and whereas some of the good people of the county of Albemarle have petitioned the General Assembly to establish in the said county a system based on the foregoing principles; be it enacted," etc. By this act the county was to be divided into districts so that no child should be more than three and one-half miles distant from a school. Each school was to be kept open nine months each year. Taxes were assessed for school purposes on the ordinary basis, except each male white person above sixteen years of age was assessed thirty cents per annum for the support of the schools.

In 1849 Virginia made the following appropriations from the Literary Fund:

1. The sum of $70,000 was divided among the several counties and those cities and towns which had corporation courts. This money was divided in proportion to white population. Those counties that had adopted the free school system applied their *pro rata* to supplement the amount raised by taxation. In case a county voted to adopt the free school system, the law required that "the Board shall establish a school in each district in which shall be taught reading, writing, arithmetic, English grammar, and geography; and, when it is practicable, the elements of physical science and such other branches of learning as the said Board may require." The money appropriated to the other counties was put into the hands of the school boards in the respective counties to be used for the exclusive purpose of educating the poor children in the private schools nearest them.

2. The law directed that the sum of $15,000 should be appropriated to the University of Virginia, and $1,500 to the Virginia Military Institute. The law stated: "In case of any deficiency of the said revenue to meet all of the said annual appropriations, they shall be preferred in the order of priority in which they are named." By this law the poor children of the State had the first claim on the Literary Fund; and, in case of a deficiency, the schools for the poor were preferred over the University of Virginia in receiving their appropriations.

3. The sum of $15,000 was appropriated from the *State Treasury* to support the asylum for the blind and the deaf mutes. The very early provision made by Virginia for the education of all the poor children in the State side by side with the children of those who were able to pay tuition, and the efficiency of this method as shown by the reports of the school commissioners of Henry County, is conclusive proof of the intense and intelligent interest of the leaders of the State in popular education from the beginning. In Virginia the law required from the first that every cent of the public money for common school education should go to the education of the poor; whereas the rule in New England was to give the poor no advantages over those in better circumstances in the appropriation of money for public school education. The method of Virginia may be criticised, but the motive was thoroughly democratic. The Legislature at a very early day made provision for the adoption of the free school system by each county, and a number of counties had adopted this system in 1860.

REFERENCES.

Code of Virginia, 1819, pp. 82-90.
Laws of Virginia, 1823-1826, p. 47.
Virginia Acts of Assembly, 1844-45, pp. 19-23.
Code of Virginia, 1849.
Fiske, Old Virginia and Her Neighbors, Vol. II., p. 1.
Reports of Commissioners of Education, Henry County, Va., Clerk's Office.

CONTRIBUTIONS TO THE AMERICAN SYSTEM OF EDUCATION.

1. The idea of local public schools, as distinguished from local private schools, originated in New England.

2. The idea of compulsory education came from the North.

3. The idea of the State system of public schools, as distinguished from the local system of public schools of New England, originated in the South, and to-day is in vogue in every State in the Union.

4. The idea of a State Fund for the education of those who were not able to pay their tuition originated in the South.

5. The idea of the education of the poor children by the State came from the South.

6. The idea of the State system of State public free schools was born in the South.

7. The idea of the State university, free from all ecclesiastical bias, not in opposition but supplementary to the denominational

schools as distinguished from the ecclesiastical system of higher education in vogue in New England, was a Southern contribution.

8. The idea of the university, as distinguished from the college, first found a lodgment in the South.

Surely the Southern States have a right to feel proud of their contributions to the American system of education.

# V. POLITICAL LIFE IN VIRGINIA BE-FORE THE CIVIL WAR.

"Everywhere except in the South a broad manhood suffrage presently came to prevail." (Woodrow Wilson, D. and R., p. 112.)
"The planters were the sole repositories of political power." (W. P. Trent, "Life of W. G. Simms," p. 39.)
"Slavery created a caste among those of the ruling race in the South." (Schouler, Vol. II., p. 231.)
"Political power, like the slaves, was in the hands of a few great barons." (Andrews, Vol. II., p. 4, 5.)

The suffrage laws of Virginia for the seventeenth century have been given. In 1762, and again in 1769, the General Assembly enacted that the franchise should be extended to every man who owned fifty (instead of one hundred) acres of uninhabited and uncultivated land. But to both of these acts the English sovereign refused his approval. In 1785 the General Assembly of the State of Virginia passed the act which had been twice vetoed by the king.

In 1829 the suffrage law was again revised, and made still more liberal. The law provided that either of the following qualifications should entitle a man to vote:

1. A freehold containing twenty-five acres of improved land acquired before 1830.

2. A freehold containing fifty acres of unimproved land acquired before 1830.

3. A freehold valued at $25.

4. A joint tenantship valued at $25.

5. A reversion valued at $50.

6. A five years' leasehold of the annual rental value of $20.

This law in 1829 made suffrage in Virginia almost universal. It was claimed at the time that many of the freeholds containing fifty acres of unimproved land were worth in the mountain districts only a few cents. But even this insignificant qualification was swept away. The convention which met in 1850 gave the franchise to every white male in the State over twenty-one years of age, with no property or educational qualifications. This was the law in 1860. It is very difficult to find any traces of the ruling aristocracy—the slaveholding oligarchy—in the history of suffrage in Virginia.

The fact that a very much larger per cent of the people vote to-day than in the early days of our country does not at all prove, as some seem to think, that society is more democratic now than formerly. To-day one-half of the people of this country live in villages, towns, and cities, and hence can go to the polls and vote with practically no loss of time. And the country people now have but a short distance to go in order to reach the polls. In former times nearly every man had to travel a long distance over rough roads in order to reach the voting precincts. To-day enormous sums of money are spent on each election, and men all over the country are carried to the polls in carriages free of charge if they wish it.

### POLITICAL LIFE IN HENRY COUNTY.

Henry County, Va., contained the largest number of big slaveholders, in proportion to its population, of any county in the State, with one exception, and the big slaveholders of Henry were always anxious to hold political office. The Representatives in the Legislature and State Senate from 1787 to 1860 owned the following numbers of slaves over twelve years of age, as given by the property books of this county. The numbers are given chronologically, beginning with 1789 and ending with 1860:

6-0-5-19-8-6-5-12-7-12-8-14-3-40-3-4-0-4-2-0-5-4-1-4-0-2-0-9-16

The number of slaves belonging to General Martin, who was one of the big slaveholders and who represented the county, is not here given. One of the poor men who are given represented Henry County in the State Legislature in 1852. The total valuation of his property was less than $500. He defeated one of the largest slaveholders in the county. Another poor man represented Henry and the adjoining counties in the State Senate from 1832 to 1840.

Below is given the number of slaves owned by each justice of the peace of Henry County from 1853 to 1858:

8-0-2-2-5-1-10-9-1-6-0-5-8-8-7-6-28-19-1-2-8-2-1-0-0-6-2-0-0-3-0

Although Henry County had a large number of big slaveholders who were anxious to hold office, the poor men got their share of political honors. It may be said by some who are incapable of tracing the relation of cause and effect that the fact that the large majority of those who held office owned one or more slaves proves that slave ownership put them in office, and that those who owned no slaves could not be elected to political office. It is hardly necessary to give an answer to this. In an agricultural community like this it was perfectly natural for every fairly successful farmer to buy one or more slaves, just as the fairly successful farmer in Ohio would employ one or more men in order to increase his output. The reason that big slaveholders were often in office may be very easily explained without resorting to the puerile and absolutely unreasonable theory which has been generally accepted. As can be seen from the "Interviews," there was no prejudice on the part of the masses of the people against the big slaveholders. These men as a rule were industrious and competent, and were willing to give their services in this way. The fact that they were often elected to office proves just the opposite of what it has been made to prove by the historians. It shows beyond question that, notwithstanding the fact that they were handicapped to a certain extent in going before the people as rich men, they conducted themselves in such a way in their communities that they won the confidence and good will and support of the poorer people. They had no power whatever over the masses of the people, and hence the only possible way they could get the support of the people was to deserve it by the lives they lived. It was not slaves but merit that put these men in office, as every fact in this investigation shows.

## THE GOVERNORS OF VIRGINIA FROM 1841 TO 1861.

It has been shown that in the large slaveholding sections of Virginia poor men represented their counties in the Legislature and in the State Senate. This was certainly true with reference to those who filled the smaller offices. But were men who were poor in their youth and without great family record ever elected to hold prominent offices in the State?

The first Governor of independent Virginia was Patrick Henry. Mr. Henry was again elected Governor in 1785. He was born in 1736, and was one of nineteen children. At the age of fifteen he was placed with a country merchant. At eighteen he married the daughter of a keeper of a house of entertainment at Hanover Court House, a small country village. Mr. Henry assisted his father-in-law at the tavern. After six weeks' preparation he obtained a license

6

to practice law at the age of twenty-four. He entered the house of burgesses in 1765 from Louisa County. This was in Tide Water Virginia. The first and fourth Governor of Virginia came from the ranks of the "plain people." It would be interesting to make a study of the lives of all the Governors of Virginia in this connection, but we can give here only a brief statement of facts with reference to those who filled this high office for the two decades just previous to the Civil War. This is the period that is of greatest interest to us in this connection.

There were eight men who served as the chief executives of Virginia from 1841 to 1861. Two of these had been farm hands in their early days, and one had been a tailor. A fourth was the grandson of a school-teacher who wrote in the office of a county surveyor and acted as deputy sheriff of Botetourt Cunty. A fifth was the son of a Scotchman who came to Virginia as the employee of a milling company. A sixth was a lawyer and mail contractor, and evidently came from the "plain people." Only one of the eight who filled this highest office belonged to a prominent family; this was Gov. Henry A. Wise. One of the Governors who had been a farm hand in his early days came from Tide Water Virginia, and the other came from the territory now included in the State of West Virginia. The Governor who had worked at the tailor's trade in his early days was the son of a butcher, and came from the "aristocratic" town of Lexington, situated in the richest section of the Old Dominion. This was the home of Stonewall Jackson before the Civil War, and the home of Gen. Robert E. Lee after the war.

REFERENCES.

Henning's Statutes, Vol. II., p. 204.
Chandler's History of Suffrage in Virginia.
Old Almanacks, Virginia State Library and Virginia Historical Society, 1774-1860.
Land and Property Books in the counties of Henry and Bedford, Va.
Lives of the Governors of Virginia, Virginia Historical Society.
Various Documents in Clerk's Office of Henry County, Va.

# VI. THE MORAL LIFE OF THE PEOPLE FROM A STUDY OF CRIME AND PAUPERISM.

"Their moral condition [the poor whites] was groveling baseness. The government of South Carolina was in favor of doing something to elevate the poor, but feared they were hopelessly doomed to ignorance, poverty, and crime." (Rhodes, Vol. I., p. 344.)

"Their days [the poor whites] were spent in lounging about the taverns, quarreling, and gambling, and creating disturbances at elections." (McMaster, Vol. II., p. 147.)

"Many of the Southern crackers or poor whites spring from this class [Virginia redemptioners], which also in the backwoods gave birth to generations of violent and hardened criminals, and to an even greater number of shiftless, lazy, cowardly cumberers of the earth's surface." (Theodore Roosevelt, "Winning of the West," Vol. II., p. 130.)

If the great masses of the white people in the South were the most lazy, the most idle, the most shiftless, the most worthless of men, we should naturally expect to find a much larger per cent of criminals and paupers in this section than in the North. But when we turn to the census reports we find just the opposite:

| | Southern States. | New England States. | United States not Including Southern States. | New England States, Massachusetts Excepted. |
|---|---|---|---|---|
| Free native-born population........ | 7,600,837 | 2,665,954 | 15,461,463 | 1,694,993 |
| Number native-born criminals convicted during one year........... | 3,614 | 6,227 | 29,152 | ........ |
| Number native-born criminals for each 100,000 native-born population | 47.5 | 232.2 | 188.5 | ........ |
| Number free native-born paupers supported within one year......... | 17,967 | 34,427 | 140,789 | 16,417 |
| Number free native-born paupers for each 100,000 population........... | 223.3 | 1,249.7 | 910.5 | 962.6 |

In the older States we naturally expect to find a larger number of paupers than in the new. The weak and disabled stay behind, while the strong and vigorous move into new sections. The older Southern States should be compared with the New England and other older States of the North, rather than with the Western States, with reference to the relative numbers of paupers. Whether we take the agricultural sections of New England or the town sections, we see that the relative number of native-born paupers was far in excess of the number in the South. Vermont did not have a single city in 1860, whereas Virginia had six cities with a population of over 100,000, and yet Vermont cared for nearly twice as many native-born paupers in proportion to her population; yet Virginia had more than 50,000 free negroes in 1860, who furnished a large proportion of the paupers charged to this State.

A larger number of native-born people were convicted of crime in Massachusetts in one year than in all the fourteen Southern States combined. Massachusetts had almost as many of her native-born population in prison in 1860 as all the Southern States combined. Maine, with about one-half of the population of Virginia, and with about the same per cent of her population living in cities, had nearly three times as many of her native-born population convicted of crime within one year as Virginia, and had a large number of her population in prison in 1860. In proportion to population, Maine had about five times as many of her native-born population convicted of crime as Virginia, and more than twice as many criminals in prison as were in prison in Virginia.

In the report of the overseers of the poor for Henry County, Va., for 1857, we find that there were six free negroes and fifteen white people cared for during the year. In 1860 nine white people and five free negroes were cared for in the almshouse of Henry County. In 1860 the white population of Henry County was 6,773. During this year only nine white people (really eight, since one was an infant) were cared for in the almshouse. If the great masses of poor white people were degenerates, it is most remarkable that we find but nine out of a population of nearly 7,000 cared for by the county in a whole year. The average number of native-born paupers in New England at this time for a population the size of the population of Henry County was 84.59. New England in 1860 had more than nine times as many native-born paupers in proportion to population as Henry County.

As has been shown, only about one-third of the white men of Henry County owned slaves. Hence two-thirds of the white population belonged to the class designated by the historians as "poor whites." Here these poor whites lived side by side with the big slaveholders, and hence were the "unfortunate victims" of the many "inhuman curses" that came to them from such an environment.

If the county provided for paupers, we would naturally expect to find a long list of this class in the almshouse. That the county did make ample provision for paupers, we are absolutely certain. The fact that a number of free negroes were found in the almshouse, and were cared for by the county, is positive proof that there was not a single white person in the county turned away. The free negroes were not desirable citizens in the South before the war, and certainly these would not have been preferred by the county's authorities over the whites. In 1860 this county had a free negro population of about 200, and a white population of nearly 7,000. The whites of this year furnished nine of their number to the almshouse, while the free negroes, out of a population of 200, contributed five. In 1857, when the free negro population was perhaps less than 200, they contributed six of their number to the almshouse. Virginia in 1860 had 50,000 free negroes; and if the free negroes of Henry County were representative, it is very clear that the pauper list of Virginia was made up very largely of free negroes.

REFERENCES.

Eighth Census of United States, Vol. Population, pp. 516-518.
Reports of Overseer of Poor, Henry County, Va., Clerk's Office.
Eighth Census of United States, Vol. Mortality, etc., p. 512.

# VII. PERSONAL INTERVIEWS WITH MEN WHO LIVED UNDER THE OLD REGIME.

In the summer of 1902 a number of interviews were had with old citizens of Henry, Franklin, Pittsylvania, and Bedford Counties, Va. All of the men interviewed were grown men in 1860, and a number of them had reached middle age at that time. All of these men were interviewed by the writer "face to face." In each case the writer tried to get the real facts as they were remembered by these gentlemen. The answers to the questions in every case were written down as they were given, in the presence of those questioned. With one exception, the writer did not know the opinions of any of these gentlemen with reference to the questions asked before the interviews were held. In only one instance was an interview held in the presence of another, who had been interviewed by the writer before. These men lived in the midst of the big slaveholding section of Virginia, and a large majority of them lived in Henry County, preëminently the county of the big slaveholder.

## QUESTIONS ASKED.

1. Age?
2. How many slaves did you own at the beginning of the war?
3. Did you hold any political office before the war?
4. In your opinion what were the opportunities before the Civil War for a poor young man to accumulate a sufficient amount of capital to buy a farm, or to get into some other kind of business for himself, and thus become an independent citizen?
5. If a poor young man of humble origin, but of good character and of industrious habits, tried to "rise" in life, what was the attitude of the people of the community to him?
6. Was there any effort on the part of big slaveholders to keep such a man down?
7. Could they have kept him down if they had tried?
8. Was there any antagonism between the big slaveholders and the men in moderate circumstances?

9. Did you know personally any of the big slaveholders?

10. What was their attitude toward the poor?

11. In a political contest was there any effort on the part of the big slaveholders to bulldoze or intimidate the poor, or to force them to vote any particular way?

12. Was a poor man free to vote his own sentiments?

13. In a political contest between a big slaveholder and a man who owned but a few or no slaves at all, all other things being equal, did the fact that one candidate was a big slaveholder and the other held no slaves influence the voter in casting his ballot? If so, how?

14. Was it considered dishonorable then for a white man to do manual labor?

15. Was all honest work considered honorable except menial labor?

16. Did you ever know of any one who was taught to look down on honest toil?

17. What was meant by "poor white trash?"

18. Were the big slaveholders sociable? Were they inclined to converse freely with men of ordinary means when meeting them?

19. At hotels and churches and at political and other meetings was anything done to show that big slaveholders were considered better than other honest, intelligent citizens of moderate means?

## A SUMMARY OF THE INTERVIEWS.

Here we can give only a brief summary of the answers given to these questions.

The ages of those interviewed, in 1860, were as follows: 20-24-25-25-27-28-28-29-29-29-30-31-31-32-32-32-34-34-34-35-37-38-39-39-39-42.

The total number interviewed, 25.

The occupations of those interviewed before the Civil War: Farmers, 9; physicians, 3; farmers and school-teachers, 2; overseer, 1; merchant and manufacturer, 1; clerk of court, 1; lawyer, 1; factory hands, 2; harness maker, 1; blacksmiths, 2.

At least eleven of those interviewed, and perhaps more, owned no slaves. (The writer failed to get an answer to the question of how many slaves were owned before the war in a few cases.) One owned thirty slaves, two owned three slaves, and one owned one slave. One gentleman interviewed was the son of one of the largest slaveholders in the county.

Nearly all of those interviewed stated that the opportunities were

good for a poor young man to rise, that such a young man was en-
couraged by all; that there were no efforts on the part of the big
slaveholders to keep such a man down; that they could not have
kept him down if they had tried. All of them stated that the feeling was good between the big slaveholders and others in the community; that the slaveholders, as a rule, were kind and sociable; that
there was no effort on their part to intimidate the poor at elections;
that every man was free to vote his own sentiments. Practically all
state that the fact that a man owned a large number of slaves did
not help him in a political contest with a poor man. All state that
manual labor was held in high esteem, and no one ever heard of any
who was taught to look down on manual labor. At hotels, public
meetings, etc., all state that there was no distinction made between
big slaveholders and others. The term "poor white trash" was used
by the negroes to designate white people who did not own slaves.

It will be observed by a careful reading of these interviews that,
although these men represent every sphere of life, and were interviewed separately, with one single exception, there is not a single
vital point of difference between them. We have here men who
were working at the blacksmith's trade, school-teachers, poor farmers, professional men, and men belonging to the most prominent
families, all giving practically the same testimony. The fact that
all of these men virtually agree on every point makes their testimony
the very strongest possible. Their statement of facts must be accepted as true beyond question; their generalizations must be judged
in the light of their opportunities and capacities for interpreting the
life of which they speak.

### CONCLUSION.

The results obtained from these separate and distinct lines of investigation are practically the same, and in the estimation of the
writer warrant the following conclusions:

1. The slave aristocracy, or the slave oligarchy, described by the
historians as existing in Virginia before the Civil War, really had
no existence save in the minds of these writers. Probably no purer
type of a sane white democracy has ever been known in America
than that which was in existence in Virginia in 1860.

2. There was no more a land and slave aristocracy in Virginia before the Civil War than there was a land and horse aristocracy in
Ohio, or a land and factory aristocracy in Massachusetts.

3. The opportunities were no greater in Virginia—and certainly the inclination was no greater—for the few strong men to get a monopoly on all the best land than in Ohio, New York, or New England. As a matter of fact no such monopoly was in existence in any large agricultural section in this country before the Civil War, and was absolutely impossible in a country the size of ours, and with such a limited population.

4. The economic conditions in Virginia were no more favorable to the accumulation of wealth without diligence, industry, and close business management on the part of the directors than in Ohio, New York, or Massachusetts.

5. The conditions of life in New England and in the Middle Northern States furnished opportunities as adequate for a leisure class as did the conditions of life in Virginia.

6. The poor man in Virginia before the Civil War had as good an opportunity to rise as the poor man in any of the other older States where agriculture occupied the same relative position to other industries as in Virginia.

7. The statements made by historians and by other writers that the white people of the South of all classes were too proud to do manual labor is utterly groundless, and in light of the facts these statements are ridiculous. Manual labor has been engaged in by the great masses of the whites of the South, and has been honored by all, from the beginning of our history down to the present day.

8. The picture given by the historians of the typical life of the Virginia planter and of the Virginia "poor whites," living in idleness, sloth, and debauchery, is supported by no fact. As a matter of fact the great masses of the white people of Virginia and of the whole South stood second to the people of no other section of this country in diligence, industry, and frugality.

9. The statement persistently and boldly made by almost every one who writes or speaks on this subject that the industrial conditions in the South in 1860 were virtually the same that they were in the beginning of the republic, that the South was exclusively agricultural and was prevented from any other kind of development by the institution of slavery, is without any basis of truth whatsoever, and is at once set aside by simply opening the census reports of 1860. The South was engaged in almost every kind of manufacturing carried on in this country in 1860, and had nearly as much capital in-

7

vested in manufacturing on Southern soil in 1860 as all the New England States had in 1850; and New England was a manufacturing center from the beginning.

10. The idea that the South was on a decline industrially or in any other way from 1850 to 1860 is contradicted by every page of the census of 1860. Every reliable fact that can be had indicates that the development and progress of the South had never been greater in any decade of its history than it was between 1850 and 1860, and that the progress within this period was not surpassed by any other section of this country.

11. The statement made that there was no free school system in the South before the Civil War has no foundation. There was a free school system in every Southern State before 1860, and it was developing as rapidly as any new institution could be expected to develop among a conservative people. We have every reason to believe that the free school system in the South would have been perfected twenty years earlier had it not been for the Civil War.

12. The idea that education and educational facilities in general were relatively small in the South as compared with the North, and that the Southerners showed a relative lack of interest in education before the Civil War, is absolutely contradicted by facts that should be known by every man who presumes to write history.

13. The impression made by the historians that the great masses of the poor white people of the South were thriftless, vicious, and criminally inclined is wholly unsupported except by the bare statements of these writers. The proportion of native-born criminals and paupers to the whole native-born population was sensationally less in the South than in New England or in the other Northern States.

14. In 1860 the South had by far a greater *per capita* wealth than the North, and the increase in wealth from 1850 to 1860 was greater in the South than in the North. In 1860 the South had a greater railroad mileage in proportion to free population than the rest of the country, and the increase in railroad construction was greater in the South from 1850 to 1860 than in the rest of the country. The increase in manufacturing from 1850 to 1860 was greater in the South that it was in New England. The South in 1860 was spending more money annually for educational purposes, in proportion to free population, than either New England or the other Northern States.